Lucien Malson

Jean Itard

NLB

Wolf Children

The Wild Boy of Aveyron

Les enfants sauvages first published by
Union Générale d'Éditions 1964
© Union Générale d'Éditions 1964
This translation first published 1972
Translated by Edmund Fawcett, Peter Ayrton and Joan White
© NLB 1972

NLB, 7 Carlisle Street, London, w 1

Designed by Gerald Cinamon
Typeset in Monotype Ehrhardt
and printed by
Western Printing Services Ltd, Bristol

Wolf Children LUCIEN MALSON

The Wild Boy of Aveyron JEAN ITARD

Acknowledgment: I am grateful to M. Fourgon, Director of the Institution Nationale des Sourds-Muets, for allowing me access to its archives and to Itard's manuscripts, many of which remain unpublished.

L.M.

Wolf Children

Lucien Malson

Introduction
Wolf Children
and the
Problem of Human Nature

The idea that man has no nature is now beyond dispute. He has or rather is a history. Why this theory should have caused such a scandal when it was advanced by the existentialists a few years ago is still not clear since it is now the explicit assumption of all the main currents of contemporary thought. Behaviourists deny that 'mental characteristics or intellectual skills and capacities can be inherited'. Marxism recognizes that 'man at birth is the least capable of all creatures' and that this is 'the pre-condition of his further progress'. Psycho-analysis, in the words of Lagache, confirms that 'there is nothing in human beings to suggest the presence of instincts with their own patterns of development'. That current which combines elements from both Marxism and psycho-analysis – culturalism – dispels any remaining doubts on this issue by revealing just how much the individual owes to the environment in the construction of his personality.

The notion of instinct itself has admittedly lost much of its former rigidity even in animal psychology. The learning of skills by imitation among the higher animals, and the influence of group suggestion among the lower animals which live in a sort of permanent hypnosis, are now recognized as evidence of the important part which the environment plays in the shaping of the instincts. But the instincts are still treated nevertheless as a sort of '*a priori* of the species' whose directions each member has to follow, even when separated prematurely from the group.

The behaviour of animals is to this extent based on something like a nature. Complete isolation of the human child, on the other hand, reveals the absence of these dependable *a priori*, of adaptive schemata peculiar to the species. Children deprived too early of all social contact – those known as feral or 'wolf' children – become so stunted in their solitude that their behaviour comes to resemble that of the lower animals. Rather than a state of nature in which one can detect a rudimentary *homo sapiens* or *homo faber*, one discovers instead a condition of such abnormality that to understand it one needs not psychology, but teratology.

The fact is that human behaviour does not depend on heredity to the same extent as animal behaviour. The system of biological needs and functions carried by the genotype and passed on to man at birth relates him to all other living creatures rather than defines him as specifically human, and it is this very absence of predetermined characteristics which means that man's possibilities are unlimited. Man's is not a closed life, ruled and governed by a *given nature*, but an open one. He creates and imposes order on an *acquired nature*. This is why there has emerged under the pressure of cultural circumstances a variety of social types which diversify man in time and space, and why there is not just a single type with the character of a species. If one studies the similarities between men one will find that what they have in common is a structure of possibilities, or rather of probabilities, which are only realized in some specific social context. Before his encounter with others man is nothing but a notional quantity as thin and insubstantial as mist. To acquire his substance, he requires a milieu – the presence of others.

It is pointless to speculate on the precise origins of mankind; one must accept that before the appearance of a *single* man, there must have existed a proto-human society – a society before being – in which 'mutants' could develop. The exact nature of these mutations, which figure in the theory of evolution and which are presupposed by psycho-sociology, is not clear. Nevertheless of this much we can be certain: there exists today a being which, unlike everything else in the world, does not appear at birth as a 'prefabricated system' but which has still to be constructed and has everything to learn. Anything endogenous, anything that can be attributed to this being's own faculties or to its native dispositions has, it must be stressed, the substance of a mist.

The gradual rejection of the idea of human nature was obviously connected with social and economic changes and can be given political or cultural explanations. It can also, however, be justified scientifically and it is this justification which will be examined here.

The problem of human nature is the problem of psychological heredity. For though it is perfectly plain that man can inherit biological characteristics, when one examines the area in which he displays his peculiarly human qualities – thought and emotion and their consequence, action – it is extremely doubtful whether there is anything here which is genetically transmitted. The natural in man is due to inborn heredity, the cultural to his acquired heritage. Congenital heritage is received during gestation, perinatal and postnatal at the moment of birth, and throughout human education. Even in the purely organic sphere it is difficult to draw the line between what is natural and what is cultural. The size and weight of a child for instance depend not only on hereditary factors but also on favourable living conditions which in turn depend on the way of life and on the level of civilization. If food, light and warmth – not to mention affection – are missing, then the proper pattern of growth will be seriously disturbed. In the domain of psychology it becomes frankly impossible to make any sharp distinction between nature and culture. Nevertheless, it is clear that the conditions for the existence and development of biological life are physical and external whereas the forces which shape man's psychological life are social ones.

With animals (and this becomes less and less clear the higher one moves up the scale from the lower species) behaviour is confined to bodily patterns of stimulus and response. Psychological heredity here is really the same thing as instinctual heredity. With man, on the other hand, the concept of psychological heredity is devoid of sense, if one means by it the transmission of innate ideas, feelings and desires by some organic process or other.

The acceptance of the anti-naturalist point of view was made possible by the scientific study of man. Once the notion of the hereditary determination of mental characteristics, either by the individual or by the species, was exposed to rigorous and objective examination, it lost any suggestion of truth and joined other pre-critical concepts in the museum of legend and myth. To question whether an individual can inherit psychological characteristics seems, on the face of it, to pose less of a threat to traditional ways of thought than to question whether the species itself can inherit these properties. For even after the first notion has been queried one is still left with the theory that there are present in the embryo certain mental predispositions which are common to the species or to man in general. To call in question this second idea is a far greater challenge to traditional prejudice and a far more radical way of destroying the notion of human nature. This is where anti-naturalist trends in scientific thought met the sharpest opposition from orthodox opinion.

The critique of individual psychological heredity has been pursued in two different but related fields: the sociology of the family and the study of twins. The critique of generic psychological heredity has also been mounted on two fronts: cultural anthropology and the analysis of children in complete isolation. It is this last area which is the least well-known and the one for which the available source material is mostly German or Anglo-Saxon. It is on this that we will concentrate. But first we must summarize certain basic findings which will help to clarify and lend support to the ideas which will emerge from our own study. We will use the current evidence on mental heredity as additional proof. It points towards our own conclusion that the search for human nature among 'wild' children has always proved fruitless precisely because human nature can appear only when human existence has entered the social context.

phrase 'psychological inheritance' denotes a reified abstraction, a hypostasis, a fetish pure and simple. Man's only real inheritance is biological. The range of actions of which he is capable is indeed limited by a fixed set of physical dispositions, yet, by themselves, his bodily states and their changes are quite meaningless. They are only given a sense by the image of himself which he takes from his cultural milieu. Since his behaviour depends, therefore, on the intersection of purely physical events with a self-image which is cultural in origin, it cannot be explained solely in terms of his 'biological inheritance': mental constraints or catalysts always intervene between the two.

Though this conclusion is demonstrated very clearly for the human sciences, genetics remains uncertain on the issue and while one might have expected a decisive answer from it the reverse is true. Geneticists are, first of all, unable to experiment directly on human subjects and so work with the large samples that are available with the prolific and short-lived fruit-fly. They are, moreover, always suspicious of legal consanguinity. And there are other difficulties. The complexity of the psychological facts in question makes it impossible to break them down into distinguishable traits each of which could be transmitted by a particular gene. The number of genes involved must be reckoned in hundreds and this is before account is taken of the possible combinations which result when independent variables are considered. Moreover, though the Mendelian theory is still applicable to this field, it does not make any distinction in practice between inherited and acquired characteristics – in particular between the hereditary and the congenital. The relationship between the genotype and the phenotype is governed by the capricious workings of the laws of mutation, of single or double heredity, direct or crossed, associated or sex-linked, atavistic or accumulated, and by the principles of recessiveness or dominance and of relative strength and expressivity. One has only to consider these difficulties to realize the uncertain state of modern genetic studies. In fact genetic theories of the inheritance of psychological characteristics are seldom based on observations or experiments with chromosomes. They are more often *a posteriori* mathematical constructions designed to interpret the statistical results of sociological inquiries. Though this is not the place to examine the methodology, one should at least be cautious about the value of material acquired in this way.

The study of genetics brings us to the sociology of the family and a critical survey of its findings. What progress has been made in this field? The growing number of case studies has concentrated for the most part on genius and on its opposite, mental backwardness. Much has been made, as far as genius is concerned, of celebrated families: the Bernouillis (mathematics), the Darwins (biology), the Jussieus (botany), the Says (economics), not to mention the Palestrinas, Couperins, Scarlattis, Mozarts and Haydns. The most familiar example is the Bach family: of 136 members, traced through eight generations, about fifty turned out to be artists of one kind or another. It used to be thought that such a wealth of talent must be due to some particular gift which was handed down from generation to generation. But this facile assumption is nowadays rejected. A family is not just a group of people with the same biologically determined possibilities. It is an educational milieu in which force of habit and imitation of the parental example can themselves create a family tradition of specialization in some field. To be born a Bach was to be born a musician just as to be born the son of a shoemaker or financier meant that one was destined to mend soles or make one's way in a bank.

There is in fact only really ever one true genius in each family. One would never pay such attention to the other less distinguished members were it not for the eminence of the one genius. Take the Corneille family for instance: Thomas was not Pierre, but his works gain from the reflected glory of his brother's finer drama. Why did the compilers of lists of famous men never include that parallel line now obscured in the darkness of history – their brothers? If one treats the occurrence of more than one celebrity as evidence for the transmission of skills, then one should be prepared to accept cases where only one brother is well-known as equally convincing evidence to the contrary. One must in any case distinguish different fields of success. It is easier for a Rothschild to keep his father's clients' bank accounts than for a Mauriac to retain his father's readership.

The names in successful businesses change far less often than the names associated with intellectual success and this is just one indication that the advantages derived from a man's social position – the sons of artists and intellectuals have such a thing as well – are greater if the father's investments have been material rather than intellectual. Galton is quoted as having remarked quite seriously that 'the heredity-chances of becoming famous are twenty-four times greater for a child with a famous father'. He was probably unaware of the damning criticism which he was making of a social order – or rather moral disorder – which fixes the odds at twenty-four to one against an incompetent's losing his fortune regardless of how badly he handles it.

Moving on from psychological normality and intellectual success, what can be learnt from the study of backwardness and mental deficiency? Goddard made a careful examination of the case of Martin Kallikak who towards the end of the eighteenth century fathered an illegitimate son with an innkeeper's daughter and so started two parallel lines of descent. The members of the recognized line were psychologically normal while the unofficial line was full of mental defectives.[1]

Anna Anastasi has asked what would have happened if the members of the bastard line had been brought up in conditions similar to those of the 'real' family. Her question is completely abstract. Rejected by society, the Kallikak's 'poor relations' were marginal elements and the fate they suffered was the only one which the manners and morals of the time allowed.[2]

Similar thoughts might arise through reading Dugdale who cites another eighteenth-century case – that of Max Jukes, a drunken vagabond from New York. Among his descendants, who by 1915

---

1. H. H. Goddard, *The Kallikak Family* (Macmillan, New York 1913).
2. Anna Anastasi, *Differential Psychology*, 3rd edn (Macmillan, New York 1962).

numbered 2,094, were counted 140 convicted criminals (seven of whom were murderers), 300 prostitutes, 310 beggars, and 600 cretins. One can imagine what a party must have been like in the Jukes's household or what sort of lesson in survival a normal child would have received in this bizarre company.[3]

There are numerous psychological studies which underscore the preponderant influence of the environment. Conrad and Jones have shown that there are greater psychological similarities between mothers and daughters than between fathers and sons. This is surely because daughters are constantly with their mothers in the house and so take them as their example. In a study by Freeman, Holtzinger and Mitchell attention is drawn to the fact that the resemblance between separated brothers varies inversely with the age at which they were separated. It is also pointed out that in families where there are several children each adopted from different parents the psychological likenesses between the real children and the adopted children are no greater or less than the likenesses between the adopted children themselves. It has been argued that because adoption agencies tend to send children to foster homes which are as much like the original home as possible, one must therefore be dealing here with a biased distribution. Admittedly, in his new family the foster child will inevitably find either foster parents of the same 'biological worth' as his natural parents or a social milieu of the same kind as his own, and so the point of the experiment might seem to be cancelled out to some extent, but as soon as cultural differences are introduced, psychological differences appear as well, and the degree of resemblance between brothers brought up separately drops on their scale from 39 to 28.[4]

Researchers like Cattell have interpreted the high correlation obtained in intelligence tests on brothers as evidence of the existence

---

3. Richard L. Dugdale, *The Jukes, a Study in Crime, Pauperism, Disease and Heredity* (New York, London 1884).

4. H. S. Conrad and H. E. Jones, 'A Second Study of Familial Resemblances in Intelligence', *Yearbook for the Study of Education* (Public School Publishing Corporation, Bloomington, Indiana 1940). Freeman, Holtzinger and Mitchell, 'The Influence of the Environment on Intelligence', *Yearbook for the Study of Education* (ibid., 1928).

of hereditary dispositions of some kind. They make the naïve mistake of assuming that all cultural and educational bias can be eliminated from these tests and that they are therefore capable of revealing the powers of 'pure thought'.[5] There are no such things as mental constructions which do not have to be constructed or ways of thinking which do not require operational schemata for their articulation. Even non-verbal tests presuppose mental habits of some kind. This is why all the significant correlations can be readily explained by appeal to the environment. If 'reciprocal mental retardation' diminishes with the degree of kinship then this must be taken as another indication of the extent to which it depends on similarity in upbringing. Conversely, the children of retarded parents are almost always themselves retarded, precisely because they face a two-in-two chance of finding a model of backwardness in their immediate environment.

One finds further support for the culturalist hypothesis in Penrose's finding that the reciprocity of cretinism is three times higher between mother and child than between father and child. In our society the mother plays an educational role which brings her into closer contact with the child. She embodies and symbolizes the primacy of the environment.

The same is true in the domain of nervous illness where, as Crook has pointed out, the relations of 'autonomy' and 'dominance' tend to hold between the child and its mother rather than its father who is more 'distant'.[6] In the emotional sphere the importance of one's acquired heritage in comparison to one's basic heredity is perhaps even clearer than in the intellectual sphere.

There are other experimental results which point to the same conclusion. According to Richardson, the coefficient of correlation in their intelligence tests between husbands and wives was found to be as high as it was between brothers and sisters.[7] The possession of

5. R. Cattell, 'A Culture-Free Intelligence Test', *Journal of Educational Psychology*, no. 31, 1940, pp. 161–79 and no. 32, pp. 81–100.

6. M. N. Crook, 'A Measurement of Personality', *Psychological Record*, 1, 1937, pp. 479–502.

7. S. K. Richardson, 'The correlation of Intelligence Quotients of siblings of the same chronological age levels', *Journal of Juvenile Research*, 20, 1936, pp. 186–98.

a common genotype does not seem to increase the resemblances which develop anyway between people who live together. Bayley and Van Alstyne claim that the intellectual level of the parents is a far better guide in predicting the intellectual ability which their child will show at the age of ten than any of the tests carried out in infancy at a time when the role of the environment is still allegedly negligible and the child therefore 'closer to himself'. According to Skeels, once the children of mentally retarded mothers are adopted by 'normal' families they can reach IQ levels at least as high as the average for the population as a whole.[8] This finding confirms the work of Freeman, Holtzinger and Mitchell who showed in their study of adopted children that the ones with retarded parents did not reveal any characteristic mental defects.

The racist claim that blacks are intellectually inferior to whites is not borne out by the findings of Ruth Benedict and Gene Weltfish that blacks educated in the North show consistently higher scores in IQ tests than whites educated in the South.[9]

In his standard book on psychology, Carmichael attempts to explain this by appealing to the notion of 'selective migration'. According to this theory only the most resourceful and gifted blacks can find the means to leave the South for parts of the USA where segregation is less rigid. There would hardly be any point in saying anything further about this absurd hypothesis were it not for the amount of evidence which so unequivocally refutes it. Much of this can be found in Otto Klineberg's educational and social study of blacks who left the South. He shows that it was not the most intelligent or best-endowed who fled the stifling atmosphere in which they found themselves but if anything the reverse, and that therefore the notion of selective migration is quite groundless.

One might note in passing that racism itself is based on the theory that behaviour is determined by inherited physical characteristics.

---

8. H. M. Skeels, 'Mental Development of Children in Foster Homes', *Journal of Genetic Psychology*, no. 49, 1936, pp. 91–106.
9. Ruth Benedict and Gene Weltfish, *Race: Science and Politics* (Viking Press, New York 1947), p. 75.

In so far as the racist theory invoked the statistical frequencies of transmitted characteristics in families of particular types, it may have seemed like a variant – less exact perhaps – of the theory of psychological heredity. It is today no more than obsession, the product of anxiety, the pathological view of those blind to argument.

The family is a cultural milieu as well as a set of chromosome parcels. The weakness of all previous discussions of this subject was that when it came to defining the family or the ethnic group this fact was conveniently ignored. People treated the matter as a purely biological problem. This is why in social psychology the final answer must be sought in the systematic study of twinship. The study of genetics led to the sociology of the family because it was there that tests could be found for its theories. The sociology of the family leads in its turn to the study of twins, and though it may not be obvious the reason for this is quite simple. There are two sorts of twin: fraternal and identical, and it is this difference which provides the opportunity for a 'decisive test' – if such a thing were possible. Identical or monozygotic twins develop from a single egg which divides in the womb after fertilization, and so they share the same chromosomic inheritance. Fraternal twins, on the other hand, are the result of the separate fertilization of two distinct eggs and so from the genetic point of view have nothing more in common than ordinary siblings.

With these definitions clear, the case now clearly presents itself: both sorts of twins must be affected by their environment in the same way; if therefore one can show that the psychological resemblances between identical twins are greater than between fraternal twins then one will have demonstrated by a process of isolation the influence of the genotype. Since hereditary and environmental factors are for the purposes of this theoretical experiment clearly distinguishable, one should be able to deduce the influence of the one from that of the other by the simple operation of subtraction.

A large number of experiments in this field have been conducted by psychologists particularly on the question of intelligence. One fact stands out: identical twins show far fewer psychological than physiological similarities. Whether or not two identical twins have been educated together obviously bears little relation to statistics relating, for example, to the size of their heads. The reverse is true of their intelligence quotients. One is faced from the start with the problem of deciding the relationship between the psychological and the physiological, avoiding of course a simplicist determinism which treats them as cause and effect. The racist theories of the nineteenth century, according to which intelligence depended on the shape of the skull, collapsed with the progress of anthropological studies (the Kaffirs for instance turned out to be just as dolichocephalic as the northern Europeans), and in the face of psychology itself (the more gifted students in American universities were not found to have noticeably narrow skulls). It is true that if one compares one species with another it is possible to detect a relationship between brain weights and the level of intellectual development. But such relationships cannot be discovered within a species. One cannot, admittedly, rule out the existence of subtler forms of conditioning of the kind to which people allude when they talk about 'nervous weakness' or the effects of 'the glands'. But here again it must be stressed that though mental life does undoubtedly depend on organic factors, organic life itself depends on the subjective existence of the individual considered as a whole. It was for a long time thought that the 'tranquillity' and 'wisdom' of the Chinese was due to the possession of a metabolism much slower than our own. In fact it speeded up considerably among those who went to San Francisco just as it slowed down among westerners who made long stays in the Far East. The complexity of the relationship between the mind and the body is shown very clearly in the clinical treatment of neuroses, particularly of those in which the patient is able to make himself ill in any way he wishes. Psychosomatic medicine underlines the psychological origin of peptic ulcers and of certain types of eczemas. Because there are never 'purely psychological' cases or 'purely physiological' cases it is a mistake to interpret a close correlation of psychological and physiological findings as evidence for the working of a linear causality. What it shows rather is that the two are inter-dependent. This should explain why in the case of identical twins brought up apart one does not find the simple one-to-one fit between their organic inheritance and their patterns of behaviour which traditional theories would have led one to expect.

Considering all cases, are identical twins more alike than fraternal twins? It certainly seems so at first sight, particularly in the sphere of intelligence. Nevertheless one must be careful when examining the results because they tend to vary according to whether the tests used are verbal or not and according to differences between ob-servers. Newman, Freeman and Holtzinger found very similar degrees of difference in IQ scores between fraternal twins (9.8) and identical twins brought up in isolation from each other (9.9). The case cited by Newman of a monozygotic pair whose scores varied by as much as a third of the mean (97 and 130) could only be explained by some peculiarity in the life of one of the twins.[10]

Research into 'character' turns out to be less straightforward. Early attempts were made to study criminal twins despite the vagueness of the notion of criminality invoked. Lange's *Verbrechen als Schicksal* which first appeared in 1929 based its findings on a study of only thirty cases.[11]

Robert Weill reports that in 1959 studies were made of 222 pairs of twins divided evenly into 111 uniovular pairs and 111 binovular pairs. Both twins turned out to be criminal in eighty of the pairs from the former group – the identical twins. Among the fraternal twins there were only thirty-eight pairs (or 34 per cent of the cases considered) in which both members of each pair were criminals. The incidence of reciprocal criminality among ordinary siblings was only 8 per cent. Even here the working of the environment may be detected. From the genetic point of view fraternal twins are no more alike than siblings. Why then are cases where both are criminal far

10. H. H. Newman, F. N. Freeman and K. J. Holtzinger, *Twins: a Study of Heredity and Environment* (University of Chicago Press, 1939).
11. Johann Lange, *Crime as Destiny: a Study of Criminal Twins*, English translation by C. Haldane (London 1931).

more common among the one rather than the other? It is obviously because children who are physically alike tend to be made more so by their upbringing while the reverse is true of children who are physically dissimilar.

The many intellectual and emotional differences which can be found between the members of twin pairs completely undermine the old theories of hereditary determinism. For the explanation of any difference always takes the form of a dilemma: either the hereditary make-up of two uniovular twins is equally favourable to both and therefore the intellectual or emotional backwardness of the one can only be explained by appealing to external factors; or the hereditary make-up of the pair is equally unfavourable to both and therefore the escape of the one must again depend on external factors. In either case, heredity alone cannot provide a satisfactory answer.

An examination of identical twins from a psycho-social point of view clarifies the matter considerably. Identical twins are recognized by their facial resemblance to each other – by the colour of the eyes, shape of the ears, colour and distribution of hair and shape of head. The existence of one placenta and one after-birth is only an indication that twins are identical and is not a decisive test. The evidence for monozygoism is not only physical resemblances between the twins but also the resemblances which have been forced on them by their upbringing: the environment tends to treat alike those who appear to it as indistinguishable. One should not be surprised, therefore, if studies of this sort lead to conclusions already assumed in their basic premises, especially when they are confined to areas in which the role of education is particularly important such as criminality and delinquency. But despite the effect which the attitude of a third may have of imposing a certain uniformity on the members of a pair, it is always possible, if one looks carefully enough, to discover some difference between them. This was already recognized in the case of the original Siamese twins, Chang and Eng, whose extraordinary adventures were well-publicized in the last century. Zazzo has remarked perceptively that one has here to 'invert one's perspectives'.[12] He shows that at the deeper levels of personality identical twins escape their fixation on the pair and the confusions of the pseudo-mirror. As each twin internalizes what happens around him he discovers a role for himself which distinguishes him from the other, and although his genetic and cultural inheritance is shared he manages despite this to develop a personality which is his own.

Man's genetic inheritance is quite formless until it has been given a shape by social forces, yet the direction of these forces themselves may always be changed by the intervention of consciousness. It is as if the work of the environment in tapping man's hereditary reserves were itself controlled by the conception he has of it which is implicit in his existential choices. Heredity and environment are not two separate things to which human actions are added. They are not independent variables. They are rather two poles of a dialectic which, by giving form to a 'total luminosity', brings into being the human subject. The idea that men have psychological 'natures' is so riddled with objections that it must necessarily collapse. It is merely the imprisoning symbol of the thought of another age.

II. THE INHERITANCE OF THE SPECIES

It might seem nevertheless that each individual could still carry within him the ingrained character of his species, and that it was precisely such a 'common fund' which distinguished the human child from the offspring of the ant or monkey. In fact, the idea of a 'universal nature' stands just as much in need of critical re-examination as the idea of an 'individual nature'. Here again nothing is so suspect as the obvious. The comparatively recent development of both ethnological and historical studies has brought us face to face with 'primitive' societies and with civilizations whose nature had been misconceived. The great range of studies by American cultural

12. René Zazzo, 'Les différences psychologiques des jumeaux identiques et les problèmes de l'individuation', *Bulletin Psychologique* (Groupe d'Etudes Psychologique, Paris 1952), no. 6, pp. 111–15; see also *Les Jumeaux, le Couple et la Personne* (P.U.F., Paris 1960).

anthropologists, for example, has completely shattered any naïve certainties one may have had about man by revealing his unlimited diversity. This diversity can be grasped either synchronically or diachronically, in space or in time. The latter involves either the evolution of societies or the growth and development of children in a particular society. In the synchronic order there is a mass of evidence to suggest the absence of exact likenesses between all members of the species. This reveals the importance of education in forming the two basic elements in man's personality – his intelligence and his system of values. First of all it is from his environment that man learns what is good and what is bad, what is comfortable and uncomfortable: the Chinese have a liking for rotten eggs and Pacific Islanders will happily eat rotting fish. A pygmy will search for a fork in a tree to use as a bed, and the Japanese use wooden blocks as pillows.

Man also learns from his environment how to see and how to think about the world. In Japan, where it is considered polite to take a man for older than he looks, subjects under test conditions, even where politeness presumably does not count, continually guess too high. It is well known that the perception of colours, of movement, and of sounds is influenced by the subject's way of life. The Balinese, for example, are particularly sensitive to quarter-tones.

The same is true of memory (which is entirely thematic) and of the rest of the cognitive faculties. Man's characteristic emotional attitudes are also learnt from his environment. Among the Maoris who cry very easily tears are not shed when a traveller departs but only on his return. The Eskimos do not suffer from jealousy because, as in Samoa, they practise 'conjugal hospitality'. They consider the murder of a personal enemy to be quite normal; yet wars, in which people fight without even knowing each other, strike them as the height of absurdity. Since death is not considered cruel, the old accept it gladly and it is an occasion for rejoicing among their relations. In the Alor Islands in Indonesia it is common to tell lies for fun, and making false promises to children is the favourite adult pastime. A similar spirit of gentle torment can be found among the Normanby Islanders: mothers feeding their children will withdraw their nipples as a joke.

Concern for the old varies from place to place as well as with different socio-economic conditions. Certain Indian tribes from California used to strangle the old, while others would abandon them by the roadside. In Fiji they bury their aged alive. Respect for parents is equally liable to geographic variation. The father has command over life and death in certain parts of Togo, Dahomey and Cameroon and among the Negritos in the Philippines. But paternal authority was almost nil among the Brazilian aborigines or on the Kamchatka peninsula before the Russian Revolution. Tarahumaran children are allowed to strike and injure their elders with impunity. Among the Eskimos marriages are made by purchase. An Urabiman man from Australia can take as secondary wives the primary wives of other men, and in Ceylon they practise fraternal polyandry: the younger brothers enjoy conjugal rights with the eldest's wife. Incest is forbidden in every society but no two define it in exactly the same way or make the same prohibitions.

The affection and care of a mother for her child is completely absent on the islands in the Torres strait, and on the Andaman islands sons and daughters are offered willingly to family guests as presents in a gesture of friendship. What is considered a 'masculine' temperament here may be considered 'feminine' somewhere else. It is Tchambuli women, to take one example, who play the dominant role in the family. Finally, though animism is considered by Piaget as an indication of childish ways of thinking, it is in fact far less evident in many 'primitive' societies than it is in our own where, as Margaret Mead remarks, even adults are sometimes guilty of it.

Each people develops a life style which the individual takes – with reservations – as his standard. It is the influence of the social milieu, of the social 'model' which Margaret Mead perhaps better than any other writer has made so plain. The Balinese live a completely schizoid existence, and reveal a total indifference to the omens of good or evil. At the roots of this schizoidism is a traditionally incoherent education which alternates rewards and punishments at random. A child is comforted and cajoled and then quite suddenly abandoned and left to cry. He is constantly misled and made fun of by his elders. Gradually he begins to detach himself from this deceit-filled milieu and comes to treat the passage of time as a sequence of indistinguishable events. It appears to him as a vague continuum moving onwards without any particular direction.[13]

Man's basic creativity is expressed also in the various historical choices which different societies have made. Men have discovered very different solutions to the problems of how to feed, house, clothe and propel themselves, and they have been just as inventive in their social relations. There are some who think that it is in these historical choices that the notion of race is best illustrated; the idea, that is, of a specific biological racial inheritance. But the whole weight of anthropology is against this. In the words of Ruth Benedict, it is pure fantasy. To begin with, civilizations are mortal. There are many peoples which have enjoyed a moment of glory and then returned to obscurity. The rich and magnificent cultures of Africa disappeared in this way: the ancient Egyptians, the kingdom of Ethiopia at the beginning of the Christian era, or the Benin dynasty in the fifteenth century.

Secondly, just as social psychology has a decisive test in the case of twins educated separately, so anthropology has its own test in the study of migrant or displaced populations. Though the Zuñi and Kwakiutl Indians belonged to the same race, once separated on different reservations they developed completely different patterns of behaviour. The society of the Zuñi is quiet, peaceful, and serene. They have complex religious rituals which they consider valuable in themselves and they cultivate modesty, courtesy and affability. The society of the Kwakiutl is strained, nervous and competitive. They despise formal rituals, preferring more ecstatic cults, and they encourage aggressiveness, rudeness and arrogance.

The first is an example, as Ruth Benedict says, of an Apollonian civilization while the second is Dionysian (to use Nietzsche's word)

13. Margaret Mead (with Gregory Bateson), *The Balinese Character* (New York Academy of Sciences, 1942), p. 255.

or Faustian (to use Spengler's). The single race to which both tribes belonged produced complete contraries, which amounts to saying that the role played by race in the outcome was negligible if indeed it played any role at all. One cannot, admittedly, reject the influence of racial heredity out of hand, any more than one can decide *a priori* what the effect of the zodiac is on human destinies or the influence of Saturn's position in the sky on the boiling point of water. A great imaginative effort was expended in the past trying to prove that ethnic characteristics depended on a shared physical inheritance, yet there is absolutely nothing to show for it today. At the same time the opposite idea was posited: a 'nature' which united all men whatever their differences. This concept too has fallen by the wayside.

The proof in space is readily complemented by the proof through time. Theft and murder were encouraged by the Spartans as training in the warrior virtues. Prostitution was not considered a vice by the ancient Tartars, and the ancient Greeks did not treat adultery or suicide as crimes. The Thebans, Cretans, Persians and Gauls all venerated sodomy just as sapphism was revered in Lesbos. These findings were turned by de Sade into a justification for his own deranged hedonism, but in doing this the divine marquis was doubly mistaken: first of all, because he used an arbitrary selection of cases to construct an 'eternal' man who he claimed had been perverted solely by the influence of religion; secondly, because anyone who accepts an anthropological pluralism must face the moral question of how to choose the course which tends to promote freedom and diminish suffering, for himself and therefore for others. It is true, though, that the study of history splits into a thousand facets the single image that has been given to man.

The temporal dimension contains another demonstration of relativism: a rather more recent one which involves the study of children, and the study of the problem child. European psychology lays great stress on the phases through which a child must pass before he becomes a man. These phases are more or less marked in different cultures and their importance varies. In societies where weaning takes place slowly and gradually, the complex which usually accompanies it elsewhere may be considerably weakened or may even vanish altogether. In Trobriand the stage does not occur at all (and indeed no connection was made between libido and anality before the arrival of the white man). Freud believed that the Oedipus complex was universal, but according to Kardiner no trace of it can be found on the Alor islands where parents take a very small interest in their children, show them little affection and allow them a large amount of freedom, thus avoiding the constricting ties which are the source of later conflict.

Margaret Mead was unable to detect the complex among Mundugumor children. They are loathed by their mothers who abhor feeding them and who display their hostility in the way they carry them. The child is not held but left to hang by itself from the mother's neck. This maternal attitude contrasts sharply with the affection displayed by Arapesh or by Pilaga women in Argentina who put their children to sleep at their breast.[14] Roheim describes how Rigentara mothers in Central Australia sleep covering their children with their bodies.

A famous controversy on just this question took place between Malinowski and Ernest Jones, the orthodox Freudian, and it too concentrated on the Trobriand islanders. Malinowski showed that the Oedipus complex on Trobriand did not occur in the classic pattern. Husbands did not consider themselves responsible in any way for the birth of children and played a minor role within the family. The maternal uncle exercised such authority as there was, but obedience to one's elders was not obligatory. Girls from the age of four and boys from the age of six played sexual games together in public. What this amounted to was that sons on Trobriand were unable to treat their fathers as serious rivals for their mother's affection. Jones claimed that the Trobriand complex – hostility to one's uncle and love for one's sister – was merely a disguised form of the real complex which psycho-analysis had revealed in its

14. Margaret Mead, *Sex and Temperament in Three Savage Societies* (Routledge, London 1935), pp. 193–5.

patients elsewhere. Malinowski replied that the complete absence of any evidence which could be treated as proof of some deeper repression placed psycho-analysis beyond the realm of the observable and the demonstrable – beyond, in other words, the realm of science.[15]

Psycho-analysis today has become more sensitive to the complexity of the way in which human growth depends on the environment; it treats the stages as perhaps no more than artefacts which are cultural in origin. Lacan, while stressing that societies without the Oedipus complex are fast disappearing, agrees that the complex is by no means universal.

Much the same can be said of the phase of latency which between the ages of six and twelve leads the child from the resolution of the Oedipus complex to the 'crisis of puberty'. On Trobriand this stage cannot be found at all and even in western societies it is far less marked in the working class than it is in the middle class. Trobriand children do not seem to experience the crisis of puberty; nor do the Samoans or the Tanalans of Madagascar. A Tanalan child is allowed to own property at the age of five and attains adulthood with no perceptible crisis.

The confusions and anxieties which the adolescent experiences in western societies arise from the contradictory demands which are made on him just at the time when he is least certain of his role. The experience of puberty, besides, varies considerably with the interpretation which society places on it. According to Helen Deutsch, Merleau-Ponty used to compare the revolution of puberty with revolution itself: psychologists and historians, to understand either, must take account both of objective circumstances and subjective consciousness. The drama of puberty cannot be avoided by means of sexual education alone, since however well one understands something in advance it is always necessary to experience it at first hand.

15. Ernest Jones, 'Mother-Right and the Sexual Ignorance of Savages', *Essays in Applied Psycho-Analysis*, vol. 2 (Hogarth Press, London 1951), p. 145; Bronislaw Malinowski, *Sex and Repression in Savage Society* (Routledge, London 1960), Part 3, Chapter 1, 'The Rift between Psycho-analysis and Social Science'.

It still depends very much on the cultural milieu as to whether puberty is experienced as something attractive or terrifying.

Among many people this period is always a cause of great stress because of the symbolic importance attached to it and the initiation rites with which it is accompanied. Among the Plains Indians of North America the initiate is made to cut strips of flesh from his arms and legs, to sever a number of his fingers, or carry a heavy bundle of wood suspended by hooks from his chest. The African Nandi force the boy to undergo circumcision without flinching or crying. The pubescent girl is treated by the Carrier Indians of British Columbia as an object of contempt, driven from the tribe and forced to live in isolation for a period of three or four years. It requires very little imagination to understand how different the experience of puberty must be among the less warlike Apache where the first drop of menstrual blood is treated as a promise of abundance and fertility, and priests go down on bended knees before the young girl and ask her blessing.

It was rash to propose a system of invariant human characteristics so long as there were still parts of the world which remained un-explored, but today this enterprise carries little such risk. The preceding arguments have shown that there is no such thing as 'human nature' in the sense that there are chemical 'natures' which allow one to define a substance by its properties once and for all. Nevertheless man in society does reveal the possession of certain faculties which distinguish him unmistakably from the higher animals. We will assume for the sake of argument that it is these faculties, which man without exception has always possessed, that constitute his common inheritance. Three universal characteristics are cited by Köhler in the realm of intelligence and three by Lévi-Strauss in the emotional sphere.[16]

Take intelligence first. When human thinking is compared with that of the inevitable chimpanzee, three characteristics stand out:

16. Wolfgang Köhler, *The Mentality of Apes*, 2nd edn (London 1931); Claude Lévi-Strauss, *The Elementary Structures of Kinship* (Eyre and Spottiswoode, London, 1968), Chapter 7, 'The Archaic Illusion', p. 84.

man's thought is not restricted in time or space, he can think of an object by itself, and he possesses a certain combinatorial ability. Animal thought is restricted in space. An uncaged monkey finds it easy to get round an obstacle placed between him and his reward, but a caged monkey experiences great difficulty in using a stick in order to pull towards it an object placed out of its reach. In the first case success in the test depends only on the subject's motor abilities. In the second it depends on an ability to view the stick as something that will help to surmount the obstacle, as a substitute for the arm and as its spatial equivalent. Children perform this test with ease, while the most developed animal – the chimpanzee – succeeds only by chance.

Animal thinking is restricted in time: an anthropoid can only carry out a task when confined in its own present, when, to be more precise, it is concentrating on the immediate visual field. When an animal carries out any task – particularly one involving the use of a stick – his performance is limited by what Merleau-Ponty calls 'the need for visual contact'. The tool, as Wallon puts it, is really only 'something used on this occasion which happens to be part of the animal's immediate perceptual field'. Chimpanzees, he adds, cannot discriminate between different instruments. The higher animals are able to use tools as extensions of their limbs to achieve immediate aims but this ability depends very much on the original position of these intermediaries in relation to the goal. The monkey will only begin to break branches to make a stick when the bait is placed nearby. As it does so, it hesitates, stops and starts again, its whole performance halting and uncertain. Animals cannot therefore really be said to use tools at all. They have no stock of technical capital. No one has ever seen a monkey shoulder his bamboo stick and set off looking for some unknown prey.

Man's thinking, by contrast, is not confined to the present. Once he grasps the concept of unlimited time he is able to form the idea of God, to make tools with which to make other tools, and to develop a language which contains the notion of the possible and so enables him to express his wishes in words. It is no accident, no mere consequence of the monkey's impoverished phonetic range, that even those which have been carefully trained – by the Kelloggs, for example, or more recently by the Hayes – are unable to achieve the subtlety in communication which even a deaf mute displays, or the powers of expression which a small child reveals in his drawings.

The second set of findings we will cite from Köhler suggests that while men can form the concept of an object by itself, animals are incapable of abstraction in this way, and always give what they see its most obvious meaning. A chimpanzee will find it difficult to interpret a packing-case-seat as a possible packing-case-step if another chimpanzee is sitting on it. Put bluntly, the world always appears to animals as a system with definite values. Men on the other hand can distinguish objects from their immediate physical surroundings and so think of many different uses to which they may be put. Animals see objects as unambiguous things and always give them a single interpretation. Their world is an environment and never a universe.

The last of Köhler's findings with which we shall deal indicates that animals, unlike men, have no combinatorial abilities and cannot calculate forces. An ape finds it impossible to construct a bridge out of planks and packing cases by itself, since to conceive the bridge it would have to realize that the vertical support is as important as the horizontal span. Nor can it disentangle a rope tied round a beam or remove a ring from a hook on the wall, since to be able to do this the animal would have to see the logical connection between distinct movements, which are spatially opposed but which point logically in the same direction.

If one is right in thinking that intelligence consists in the ability to solve problems whose solutions cannot be found by routine or by *a priori* methods, then, as Merleau-Ponty says, it is wrong to speak of animal intelligence in the sense with which one uses the word of humans.

The higher apes admittedly can 'learn to learn'. Vicki, the monkey trained by the Hayes, did, it is true, manage over the space of six years to acquire the use of three words, but one would be reluctant to call this a language, even for a complete imbecile, and it should not therefore weaken the conclusion that the animal frontier is quite clearly limited as regards intellectual ability.

In the sphere of emotion, Lévi-Strauss singles out three universal human attitudes as those which distinguish men from animals: the need for rules, the desire for reciprocity and the gesture of giving. Man, in the first place, has recourse to rules in order to escape the 'intolerable burdens of arbitrariness', and he respects them simply because they are rules. Far from providing us with examples of the complete lack of order, primitive societies reveal on closer investigation the extent to which they depend on the scrupulous observation of custom and the careful attention to ritual.

In the second place, man always tries to establish contacts with other men which are governed by some sort of equivalence if not of wealth at least in his relationships. He does this according to Lévi-Strauss (citing Susan Isaacs) because once he has realized that he is not omnipotent he tries to achieve equality with others, as it is 'the lowest common multiple of all his contradictory wishes and fears'.

Third and last, by making gifts man ensures that the other becomes his partner at the same time as he renders the object exchanged more valuable. The gift is an expression of his feelings of both strength and fear. The ego is flattered by the sense of power which the exchange gives him, yet his own weakness forces him to use the gift also as a way of winning the other's loyalty.

All three are in the end just different expressions of a fundamental desire for peace, and in attempting to satisfy it men devise systems of rules with which to replace the laws of the jungle. They are thus able to establish an order which is preferable at least to their destroying each other. Man's development may well have led to a chaotic profusion of different human types, but ethnological studies have cut through this apparently impenetrable thicket and revealed, beneath the manifest contradictions, the single path which man, unconsciously perhaps, attempts to follow.

What this amounts to for the purpose of our argument is that the child inherits, as its specifically human qualities, the ability to reason and the 'recognition' of others. But these features, singled out in the writings of Köhler and Lévi-Strauss – and more generally in the writings of other contemporary sociologists and psychologists – are really nothing more than the defining characteristics of man in society. The capacity for thought and the need for an *alter ego* both presuppose a cultural environment. There is, as we will show, not the slightest hint of either of these when the child is brought up in any other sort of environment, and this brings us to our original point: while animals can be said to possess pre-social natures, the only human constants are social ones. Even when isolated from birth, animals retain quite clearly recognizable instincts, whatever other damage they may suffer in the process, and when a domesticated animal returns to the wild its old instincts reassert themselves. Nothing like this, says Lévi-Strauss, could happen in the case of human beings because 'the species has no natural behaviour to which an isolated individual might retrogress'.[17] Deprived of the society of others man becomes a monster. He cannot regress to his pre-cultural state, because such a state never existed.

When children are prematurely deprived of their human surroundings, either by accident or design, or when they are abandoned in the wild and left to survive by their own devices, they do, in fact, develop 'unnaturally'. It would be quite absurd to treat them as 'perfect examples of some earlier human stage', or as instances of natural and therefore pre-cultural man. These Tarzan-children, as Ruyer ironically calls them, have no resemblance whatsoever to Rousseau's imaginary hero.

If any further proof is needed that the term 'human nature' is completely devoid of sense, the following study of wolf children will provide it. The accuracy and authenticity of many of the accounts have admittedly been seriously questioned, and these doubts will be examined later. We will here merely ask a single question – indeed the whole of the previous discussion was leading to this one point: now that it is generally recognized that the dominant, fundamental role in the shaping of man's personality is played by his social

17. Lévi-Strauss, op. cit., p. 5.

environment, should one be surprised that a non-human environment produces semi-human children? Stories of wolf children have been known for a long time. It was only to be expected that they were treated by the believers in human nature as a serious challenge to their view of man. Their reluctance to draw the obvious consequences from these accounts arose from a reading of the evidence which refused to allow such backwardness any cause other than physical abnormality. To the pre-scientific mind a child who was unable to walk erect or who, once the original opportunity was passed, could only master a language with great difficulty appeared as a biological freak or as a sufferer from some congenital weakness. No one today would suggest that a child prematurely isolated and deprived of adult contact could be expected to walk erect like other children, display the usual talents at writing or arithmetic and behave generally like a well-bred child should. And if the psychological portraits of these wolf children strike sceptics as exaggerated, let them sit down and exercise their literary talents on the imaginary consequences of premature isolation. Itard's question was a challenge to the nineteenth century:

If it was proposed to resolve the following metaphysical problem, viz. 'to determine what would be the degree of understanding, and the nature of the ideas of a youth, who, deprived, from his infancy, of all education, should have lived entirely separated from individuals of his species'; . . . the moral picture of this youth would be that of the Savage of Aveyron . . . (p. 99 below).

Itard made a meticulous study of this 'savage' from Aveyron in two reports which are still the best known and most convincing record of such cases. More perceptive than Victor Cousin's, Itard's insights were in many ways prophetic:

I have not the least doubt, that, if we were to insulate, at the earliest period of infancy, two children . . . and were to do the same with two quadrupeds, chosen from the species of brutes, that was the least intelligent, these latter would not shew themselves much superior to the former, in the means of providing for their wants and in taking care . . . of their own preservation (p. 138 n. 10 below).

A hundred and thirty years before the Kelloggs, Itard was already talking like a modern psychologist.

Legendary and Historical Accounts

I. THE LITERATURE ON ISOLATION

When one considers that quite serious doubts have been raised about the actual existence of Homer, Socrates and even Shakespeare, it is hardly surprising that stories of isolated children have not always been taken on trust. Accounts of their lives can be found in Herodotus, the first historian, but they also figure prominently in classical mythology. Thyro was brought up among cows, Zeus was suckled by the goat Amalthea, and Romulus and Remus were nursed by a she-wolf. It was claimed, no doubt to preserve the literary symmetry, that when Rome fell to the Goths a single child survived in the ruined city by feeding from some generous foster-animal. German myths abound with stories of wild and solitary men who commune with the spirits of the dark forest; and indeed it was to such beings that German critics compared what Etiemble called the Javanese-Rimbaud, the Rimbaud-Gaspard Hauser or the 'Ur-Rimbaud' when he commented ironically on the critical appreciations of Wolfenstein and Rudolf Kurtz.[1]

Persian accounts of bear-teachers and Japanese stories about nursing monkeys are only local expressions of a recurrent fantasy, as is the fifteenth-century Dutch story about a sea maiden washed ashore by the tide at Edam who set herself up as a seamstress. Mythical stories, nevertheless, always contain an element of truth and one should try, in the manner of Frazer and Müller, to extract this true kernel from the surrounding myth. Real episodes in mythic thinking tend to be disguised as imaginary ones, and all myths from that of the flood to those of the Theban brothers involve not only metamorphoses of nature but human dramas as well. One should

1. R. Etiemble, *Le Mythe de Rimbaud*, vol. 3 (Gallimard, Paris 1961), p. 453.

hesitate, therefore, before rejecting a story just because part of it is obviously invented.

Hoaxes here are as common as they are anywhere else: every so often the press reports the discovery of yet another Mowgli waiting for his Kipling; yet to deny the value of all the accounts of premature isolation would be like rejecting all the known Vermeers just because of Van Megeren's forgeries.

To return, however, to the basic facts of these stories of isolation, the simplest way to proceed would be to present each account regardless of whether it is legendary, historical, authentic or obviously invented. Leaving aside the ancient and medieval texts one can start immediately with the eighteenth century during which for the first time a serious interest was taken in the phenomenon of living beyond the bounds of society. The discussion was inaugurated by the historian Bernard Connor, the naturalist Buffon and the philosopher Condillac.[2] It focused initially on children who had been deprived, sometimes accidentally, of a normal and continuous education. Rousseau mentions five cases in his *Discours sur l'Origine de l'Inégalité,*

These children walk on all fours and require careful instruction before they can walk upright . . . [The child from Hesse] had been taken care of by wolves. . . . He walked so like an animal that pieces of wood had to be tied to his legs for him to hold himself erect . . . on his two feet. . . . The same was true of the child discovered in the forests of Lithuania who had lived among bears. According to Abbé Condillac he did not reveal the slightest sign of reason. He walked on all fours, lacked the power of speech and uttered sounds quite unlike anything human. The young savage from Hanover who was taken to the English court some years ago had the greatest difficulty in learning to walk on two feet. . . . Two other savages were discovered in the Pyrenees running up and down the mountainside like quadrupeds.[3]

2. Bernard Connor, *Evangelium Medici: Medicina Mystica* (London 1697), p. 133 and *The History of Poland in Several Letters to Persons of Quality* (London 1698), p. 342ff.; Etienne de Condillac, *Essai sur l'Origine des Connaissances Humaines* (Amsterdam 1746), Book I, Part 2, Chapter 2, pp. 202–5; Georges Leclerq, Comte de Buffon, *Histoire Naturelle* (Paris 1774), vol. 5, Chapter 1: 'Variétés dans l'espèce humaine', pp. 181–2. English translation by William Smellie (London 1791), p. 172.

3. J.-J. Rousseau, *Discours sur l'Origine de l'Inégalité parmi les Hommes* (1st edn, Paris 1754; new edn Garnier, Paris 1962), pp. 94–6. Five examples are cited. Rousseau sup-

Four years later Linnaeus added various other examples to Rousseau's list, and towards the end of the century von Schreber and Michael Wagner reckoned the number of known cases at fourteen.[4] One of the oldest of the cases is undoubtedly the wolf-child of Hesse (*juvenis lupinus hessensis*) who was found in 1344 running wild in the woods. According to the story, a hole had been dug for him by wolves. They had carpeted it with leaves and at night would encircle him with their bodies in order to protect him from the cold. After four years of life in the wild the child neverthe-less showed signs of a sudden mental awakening. In the same year the wolf-child of Wetteravia was found in the Hardt, the forest region near Echzel in Bavaria. Once he was back in the society of humans he too made remarkable psychological progress.[5]

The first bear-child (*juvenis ursinus lithuanus*) was captured by hunters in Lithuania after it had resisted them with its teeth and

---

poses that the upright position is natural for man and that in their imitation of animals quadruped children have to overcome their anatomical nature. His view is distorted by his own image of the 'noble savage' who is intelligent, good-natured and who walks erect on his two feet.

4. Carl von Linne (Linnaeus), *Systema Naturae* (10th edn, Stockholm 1758), Book 1, p. 20. Seven cases are listed. In the 13th edn (Leipzig 1788), Book 1, p. 21, the author adds three new cases to his previous list: the Bamberg child (taken from Camerarius), the *puella campanica* and the *puella tranislana*. J. C. D. von Schreber, *Die Saugthiere in Abbildungen nach der Natur, mit Beschreibungen* (Erlangen 1775), Book 1, pp. 31–7. This gives more detailed information on each of Linnaeus's cases and adds two more. It was translated into French as *Histoire Naturelles des Quadrupèdes Répresentés d'après Nature* (Erlangen 1775), Book 1, pp. 38–43. Michael Wagner, *Beiträge zu Philosophischen Anthropologie und den damit verwandten Wissenschaften* (Vienna 1794), pp. 251–68. The cases mentioned by these authors as well as many of those cited later are all discussed in R. M. Zingg's paper 'Feral Man and Extreme Cases of Isolation', *American Journal of Psychology*, vol. 53, 1940, pp. 487–517. This is the most complete study published on the subject. It summarizes the history of the various cases, including the doubtful as well as the probable and authentic, thirty-one in all. In the first, analytical, section Zingg provides a nomenclature and in the second section constructs a portrait of *homo ferus*. There are detailed references at the foot of each page but not all are as clear or as accurate as might be hoped, particularly those to eighteenth- and nineteenth-century texts. The list has been corrected and completed on the basis of research in the Biblio-thèque Nationale, at the Muséum d'Histoire Naturelle and at the library of the École Normale Supérieure in Paris.

5. Philippe Camerarius, *Operae horarum subcisvarum* sive *meditationes* historicae *auctiores* (Frankfurt 1602), Part 1, pp. 343ff. Pistorius, *Scriptio rerum a Germanis gestarum* (Frankfurt 1613), p. 264 (included by Linnaeus and Rousseau, loc. cit.). The Wetteravia case is mentioned by von Schreber, op. cit.

claws. He would eat only meat or grass and was particularly fond of cabbages. He refused all clothing and according to Valmont de Bomarre never adjusted successfully to his new life.[6] The Irish sheep-boy was completely insensitive to the cold and again would only touch grass and hay. His case was discussed by Nicolas Tulp, the Dutch doctor whom Rembrandt portrayed in *The Anatomy Lesson*. According to Tulp, who examined the alert and agile child in Amsterdam, he had 'a flat forehead, elongated occiput, thick neck, wide tongue and a distended stomach'.[7] Towards the end of the seventeenth century there was a similar case of the calf-child from Bamberg in Bavaria (*juvenis bovinus bambergensis*). He used to take on the largest dogs and fight them with his teeth, yet he managed in the end to achieve a far higher mental level than he had on discovery.[8]

A second Lithuanian bear-child (*juvenis ursinus lithuanus minor*) reported in 1694 learnt not only to walk erect but to talk as well. The third Lithuanian child, however, never learnt to speak and remained only interested in food.[9]

In August 1717 a girl was discovered in the woods outside Zwolle in the Dutch province of Overyssel. It turned out that she had been kidnapped from her home in Kranenburg when only sixteen months old. When found she was dressed in sacking and living on a diet of leaves and grass. She became eager to communicate with others and though she never learnt to speak, she managed to understand sign language. She learnt to spin and continued this activity until her death.[10]

In 1719 there were various local reports in the Pyrenees of children who leapt around the mountainside like chamois but the written accounts are all extremely vague.[11]

6. Valmont de Bomarre, *Dictionnaire d'Histoire Naturelle* (Paris 1775), vol. 4, p. 501, under the entry *Homme Sauvage*. Cited also by Linnaeus, loc. cit.

7. Nicolas Tulp, *Observationes Medicae* (Amsterdam 1672; 5th edn 1716), Book 4, Chapter 10, p. 296.

8. Camerarius, Linnaeus, loc. cit.

9. Condillac, Rousseau, loc. cit. The third is mentioned only by Connor, loc. cit.

10. Linnaeus (1788), loc. cit.

11. Rousseau, Linnaeus, loc. cit.

There is, however, a fairly detailed literature about two further cases: Peter, the savage from Hamlin in Hanover (1724) and the girl from Sogny in the Champagne (1731). Peter of Hanover (*juvenis hannoveranus*) had been abandoned in the forest by his father, a man named Kruger. He returned to his parents' house after a year asking to be taken in again but was turned away by the proverbial cruel step-mother. He was later captured after some sailors had spotted him in a field from their boat. He was wearing the remains of a shirt and was living off plants and bark from trees. On capture he refused the bread that was offered him, preferring instead to strip the bark from green twigs and suck the sap from the raw wood. He hated his captivity and escaped many times but was always re-captured. During his sixty-eight years in human company he was, among other things, presented at the English court to George I. He came gradually to accept the wearing of clothes, developed some sensitivity to music and, although he never learnt to talk, became able to imitate the gestures of others.[12] His progress among men was negligible, however, in comparison with that of the *puella campanica*. This girl was discovered perched in an apple tree one September evening by the servants from a château in Sogny. In the ensuing chase she escaped to a neighbouring wood but was finally tempted down from her second perch by the offer of a bucket of water from which she drank like a horse. She was dressed in animal skins and was carrying a cudgel. This girl (who was later to take the name LeBlanc) had, it turned out, accidentally killed her only companion. She ran and swam with ease. Her diet consisted of birds, frogs and fish and she had a craving for rabbit's blood, which she would drink at any opportunity; her attempts to give up this particular habit were especially difficult. At first all she could do was to

---

12. *Leipziger Zeitungen*, no. 104, 1725 and nos. 17, 61, 88, 1726; *Breslauer Samm-lungen*, vol. 34, Dec. 1725, p. 659 and vol. 36, April 1726, p. 506; *Ein Brief des Hamel-schen Burgermeisters Palm* in C. F. Fein, *Entlareter Fahel von Ausgange der Hamelschen Kinder* (Hanover 1749), p. 36; *Gentleman's Magazine*, vol. 21, 1751, p. 522 and vol. 55, 1785, pt. 1, pp. 113 and 236, pt. 2, p. 851; Jonathan Swift, *Works* (London 1755), vol. III, pt. 1, p. 132; James Burnet, Lord Monboddo, *Ancient Metaphysics* (London 1784), vol. 3, pp. 57 and 367.

scratch at the ground with her nails; however the nuns at Châlons-sur-Marne, where she was placed by the bishop, contrived to teach her to speak. It was there that she was visited by the Queen of Poland who had expressed a curiosity in the strange girl. She was later transferred to the house of the Nouvelles Catholiques in Paris where an equally distinguished visitor, the Duc d'Orléans, came to see her. Somewhat later she thought she had a vocation and decided to become a nun at the convent in Chaillot, but it seems that ill-health prevented her from pursuing this course.[13]

Jean de Liège (*Johannes Leodicensis*), like Peter of Hanover, showed a more modest development. He is said to have lived outside the society of man for sixteen years and would eat only plants and grass.[14]

It seems clear that, as in the case of Tomko, a half-savage who was discovered in Hungary on the borders of Galicia in the district of Zips, the degree of later development depends to a great extent on the length of isolation, its completeness and what preceded it. To begin with, Tomko bore only too obviously the marks of his experience, displaying an insatiable appetite for raw meat and offal. He learnt nevertheless to speak Slovakian and to understand some German. He is reported to have been completely uninterested in sex and to have been subject to convulsions. Despite continual ill-health and a premature death he made remarkable intellectual progress.[15] His rival in the literature of isolation is the bear-girl of Fraumark who was recovered from a cavern in the woods in 1767, in the district of Hont in Hungary, and taken to the hospital at Karpfen.[16]

13. Charles-Marie de la Condamine, *Histoire d'une jeune fille sauvage trouvée dans les bois à l'âge de dix ans* (Paris 1755). This contains seventy-two pages of unlikely stories about Marie-Angelique Memmie LeBlanc, as she came to be called. Racine mentioned her in *Épitre II, Sur l'Homme, Poésies Nouvelles* (Paris 1747), pp. 28–9, and again in *Eclaircissement sur la fille sauvage dont il est parlé dans* 'L'Epitre II sur l'Homme', in *Oeuvres de Louis Racine* (Paris 1808), pp. 575–82. Her case is cited also by Linnaeus (1788) and von Schreber.

14. Kenelm Digby, *Two Treatises in the one of which the Nature of Bodies, in the other the Nature of Man's Soul is looked into: In Way of Discovery of the Immortality of Reasonable Souls* (Paris 1644), pp. 247–8, and Linnaeus, loc. cit.

15. Wagner, loc. cit.

16. Pierre-Joseph Bonnaterre, *Notice Historique sur le savage de l'Aveyron et sur quelques autres individus qu'on a trouvés dans les forêts à différentes époques* (Paris 1800).

At the close of the century another strange child who had lived by himself in the woods begins to appear in this literature: this was the 'wild boy' from Aveyron, as he came to be known. The importance of this case was recognized at once by Itard who, as we will see, set out to study the child at length. His first account, which was published in 1801, opened a discussion which was to last the whole of the century.[17]

Two more cases were reported a few years later but they were poorly documented. Then, in 1828, the story of Kaspar Hauser suddenly became known and remained one of the controversies of the time. His case will be dealt with in Chapter 3 below.[18]

The 'European period' is completed by the case of the Strasbourg pig-girl who had been made to squat all her life in a pigsty and so was unable to straighten her legs.[19]

17. The contemporary literature on Victor of Aveyron begins with Constant de Saint-Estève, *Rapport sur le sauvage de l'Aveyron* (2 Pluviôse an VIII, 22 January 1800), in Bonnaterre, op. cit., pp. 23–6. Bonnaterre, who knew both Linnaeus and von Schreber, was Professor of Natural History at the École Centrale de l'Aveyron and conducted the first examination of the child. One Citizen N. (Nougairolles) published a report on him in the *Journal des Débats* (5 Pluviôse an VIII, 25 January 1800). Itard's first memoir was published under the title *De l'Education d'un Homme Sauvage ou des Premiers Développements Physiques et Moraux du Jeune Sauvage de l'Aveyron* (Paris 1801); the second under the title *Rapport Fait à S.E. le Ministre de l'Intérieur sur les Nombreux Développements et l'État Actuel du Sauvage de l'Aveyron* (Imprimerie Impériale, Paris 1807). The two works were republished in Bourneville (ed.), *Rapports et Mémoires sur le Sauvage de l'Aveyron* (Paris 1894) with introductory texts by Bousquet and Delasiauve. R. Fareng's 'Le Sauvage de L'Aveyron', *Revue du Rouergue* (October–December 1959), pp. 402–17, is a careful account of Victor and of Itard's contribution to the development of educational theory. In 'Itard et son sauvage', *Les Temps Modernes*, 233, October 1965, pp. 647–63, Octave Mannoni regrets that Itard was not Freud.

18. The main source for Kaspar Hauser is Anselm von Feuerbach, *Kaspar Hauser, Beispiel eines Verbrechens am Seelenleben des Menschen* (Ansbach 1832); English translation: *Caspar Hauser*, by H. G. Lindberg (London 1833). Among other works see: S. Von Lubeck, *Über Kaspar* (Altona 1831); Elizabeth Evans, *The Story of Caspar Hauser from Authentic Records* (London 1892); Hermann Pies, *Kaspar Hauser* (1926); Jakob Wassermann, *Kaspar Hauser oder die Trägheit des Herzens-Singen* (1947); French translation, *Gaspard Hauser ou la Paresse du Coeur*, by Romana Altdorf (Club Français du Livre, Paris 1952). Verlaine seems to have been much impressed by Kaspar Hauser's story: '*Le chanson de Gaspard Hauser*' was the original title of the poem '*Je suis venu calme orphelin*' which he wrote while in prison in Brussels. There is a colloquial version of the same poem with the punning title '*La chanson du gars pas poseur*'. Verlaine returned to the theme in a scenario for a ballet called *Mémoire d'un veuf*.

19. Wilhelm Horn, *Reisen durch Deutschland, Ungarn, Holland, Italien, Frankreich, Grossbritannien und Irland*, in *Göttingen gelehrte Anzeige*, July 1831; quoted by Feuerbach.

Attention then switched to Southern Asia where the world which the British colonizers had unearthed struck them as strange and fantastic. Considering the wretchedness of life in India and the closeness there between the world of animals and the world of men, it is hardly surprising that the country should have produced more than its share of wolf children. Sleeman reported many cases of children raised by the traditional wolf.[20]

The first was a child from Husanpur entrusted to the Rajah in 1843. Captain Nicholetts reported having found a second 'savage' child in Sultampur in 1843 and Colonel Gray claimed to have found another in the same part in 1848. The first died in captivity in 1856 while the second managed to escape. In 1850 Captain Nicholetts was entrusted with the care of a child from Chupra who had been carried off by a wolf and who was recognized, six years later in 1849, by the scar on its knee. The Bankipur child, discovered by Zulfikar Khan, learnt how to communicate by means of sign language. The last of Sleeman's cases, reported by Captain Egerton, is of doubtful validity.

On their return to human society, most of these quadrupeds refused, according to Sleeman's accounts, to wear clothes and would eat only raw meat. Some would drink by lapping at the water with their tongues while others would happily share with dogs the carcass of some dead animal. There was one who finally accepted bread to eat and who could be trusted to look after cattle. Another took to smoking and even learnt how to light his pipe by himself. One might include here two European cases from Overdyke in Holland reported by Tylor in 1863. The first was a pig-boy, called Clemens, who had a particular passion for green plants and had to be re-strained whenever he got near a cabbage patch. The second was a wolf-child who got his food by climbing trees, imitating an appropriate birdcall and stealing the eggs or nestlings. Nobody could shake him of this habit.[21]

20. William Henry Sleeman, *A Journey through the Kingdom of Oude*, 2 vols. (London 1858).Major-General Sleeman was in Oudh between 1849 and 1850 fighting the 'Thugs'. He reported seven cases in all, of which at least one was based on unreliable sources.

21. E. B. Tylor, 'Wild Men and Beast Children', *Anthropological Review*, 1, 1863, pp. 21–32. Tylor was the first specialist in cases of isolation and presented the question

We return to India with the case of the wolf-child Dina Sanichar from Sekandra who was captured near Mynepuri in 1872. He had acquired the habit of gnawing at bones to sharpen his teeth and at first refused all attempts to clothe him. All that he managed to learn throughout his twenty years in human company was to stand erect, to dress himself with difficulty and to look after his own cup and plate. Like Sleeman's second case he also smoked incessantly. Another carnivorous child was discovered in 1874 and sent to the Sekandra orphanage, but did no better than Dina Sanichar. The existence of these two was reported by one Father Erhardt to Valentin Ball, as well as that of another child from Lucknow, whose fellow had been included in Sleeman's list.[22]

The aversion to clothing of any kind was shared by the wolf-child of Kronstadt. Half-herbivore and half-carnivore, he took delight in the sound of the piano but never learnt to do anything except to fill a jug of water.[23]

Four other lupine children were reported from India in the same period. The first, the Jalpaiguri child, was discovered by a missionary in 1892. The second, a great eater of frogs, was found in 1893 in Batzipur near Dalsingarai. Another child was found in Sultanpur in 1895 and was alleged to have later become a policeman. The last of these four, a child from Shajampur discovered in 1898, remained completely stunted despite fourteen years in human company. These cases were followed shortly afterwards by those of the Justedal girl and the baboon-boy from South Africa, who was captured, so it was claimed, by the mounted police.[24] Twenty years later in 1920 the

---

in the light of the new cases cited by Sleeman. The two cases he adds are from the Napoleonic period, which produced its share of abandoned children.

22. Valentin Ball, *Jungle Life in India* (London 1880); G. C. Ferriss, *Sanichar, the Wolf-boy of India* (New York 1902).

23. August Rauber, *Homo sapiens ferus oder die Zustände der Verwilderten und ihre Bedeutung für Wissenschaft, Politik und Schule* (Leipzig 1885).

24. H. Le Roux, *Notes sur la Norvège* (Paris 1895). On p. 16 he speaks of 'the little snow-hen from Justedal'. On the baboon-boy see J. P. Foley, 'The Baboon-Boy of South Africa', *American Journal of Psychology*, 53, 1940, pp. 128–33. In 'More about the Baboon-Boy of South Africa', published in the same journal for that year, pp. 455–62, Robert Zingg destroys the story and rejects the baboon-boy as a genuine case.

case was reported of Amala and Kamala, two wolf-girls adopted at Midnapore by the Reverend Singh, and made famous in his hundred and fifty page journal. These two will be dealt with in detail separately, together with Kaspar Hauser and Victor of Aveyron.[25]

In the same year the first leopard-child was discovered in India.[26] Another wolf-child, from Maïwana, was reported in 1927 and yet another from Jhansi in 1933. This child, rescued by a British officer in Gwalior, was brought up by one Dr Antia who managed to teach him to walk upright. Zingg reports a story told to him during the same period by the villagers of Cachar of a child carried off by a leopard from under the eyes of his mother while she was gathering rice in a paddy field outside the village of Dihungi. The animal's young had been killed a few days earlier and it had been prowling the village ever since. Three years later the child was found, almost blind, the skin on his hands and feet hardened. He ate small birds and raw meat and would bite and claw at anyone who came near him. He was taken back by his family and learnt to walk on two feet.

Demaison records accounts from West Africa in the thirties of a savage child living somewhere on the border between Guinea and Senegal and of a girl in Liberia called Assicia who had 'come out of the forest'.[27]

25. There is a mass of material on Amala and Kamala, much of it in magazine articles published at the time, and listed in Zingg's 'Feral Man and Extreme Cases of Isolation', (loc. cit.). The main work is *Wolf Children and Feral Man*, written in collaboration by J. A. L. Singh and R. M. Zingg (Harper and Row, New York 1942). The first report, apart from newspaper articles, by P. C. Squires, appeared under the title 'Wolf Children of India' in the *American Journal of Psychology*, 38, 1927, pp. 313–15. W. N. Kellogg published two further articles in the same journal, 'More about the Wolf-Children of India', 43, 1931, pp. 508–9, and 'A further note about the Wolf-Children of India', 46, 1934, pp. 149–50. In this latter article he summarizes the medical evidence of Dr Sarbadhicari, who made many examinations of the two girls between their capture and death.

26. E. C. Stuart Baker, 'The Power of Scent in Wild Animals', *Journal of the Bombay Natural History Society*, 27, 1920, pp. 117–18.

27. André Demaison, *Le Livre des Enfants Sauvages* (André Bonne, Paris 1953). He cites these two cases as the pretext for a romance about Assicia, hastily written and full of errors for which he excuses himself in advance by appealing to his 'literary treatment'.

A new wolf-child was reported by Hutton in 1939,[28] and the next year two cases of prolonged confinement were reported by Davis and Maxwell respectively.[29] A gazelle-child, reported by Demaison, was found in the Syrian desert in 1946, and three final cases were reported in 1954, 1961, and 1963: the controversial Ramu in India, a Persian monkey-child, and lastly a Mauretanian gazelle-child.[30]

This is the list of the cases which the reader will find in the specialist literature. We must now examine the data to discover what regularities or statistical trends emerge from these diverse phenomena. How have legend and history presented Linnaeus's *homo ferus*, *l'homme sauvage* or feral man? The first two of Linnaeus's chosen characteristics we can accept. According to the *Systema Naturae*, feral man is usually a quadruped (*tetrapus*) and a mute (*mutus*). Linnaeus also claimed that they were covered with hair (*hirsutus*), but this is a mistaken projection from a few cases. Only the second Lithuanian child, the Kranenburg girl and the Husanpur, Shajampur and Kronstadt children were noticeably hirsute. The inclusion of this characteristic is probably a literary survival, and Rousseau may have had in mind Aristotle's description of primitive man. It may also have been because particularly hairy people were presented in travelling circuses as animal men. LeDouble and Houssay's book *Les Velus* contains much interesting information on this subject.

Walking on all fours and the inability to speak can, on the other hand, be accepted as typical characteristics. The Sogny girl admittedly, as well as the second Lithuanian child, the Hungarian cases, Kaspar of Nuremberg, Victor of Aveyron and Kamala of Midnapore all developed adequate means of expressing themselves, but

28. S. H. Hutton, 'About the Wild Boys', in *The Times*, 24 July 1939.

29. The first, known as Anna of Pennsylvania, was discussed by Kingsley Davis in an article entitled 'Extreme Isolation of a Child', in the *American Journal of Psychology*, 54, 1940, pp. 554–65. The second, Edith Riley, from Ohio, studied by F. N. Maxfield, is discussed in Zingg's article from the same journal (loc. cit.). Henri Piéron discusses Anna's case in 'L'Importance de la Période Pré-scolaire pour la Formation de l'Esprit', *Cahiers Pédagogique et d'Orientation Professionnelle* (Liège 1954).

30. The first two were reported widely in the press at the time. The third is discussed by Jean-Claude Auger in 'Un Enfant-Gazelle au Sahara Occidental', *Notes Africaines*, 98, April 1963, pp. 58–61. Between September and October 1960 Auger made repeated observations of a wild child among gazelles in the region of Tiris.

these were exceptions. Almost none of the other *homines feri* ever
learnt to speak despite repeated efforts by their teachers. Many
of them, however, managed in the end to walk erect on their two
feet.

Want is the basis of all biological life and it is common to every
species. In the *Critique de la Raison Dialectique* Sartre makes need
the starting point of human life, the motive force of history. Though
this fact may be lost from view in conditions of abundance, it is
violently revealed in situations of extreme scarcity where men
become little more than hungry mouths. It is not surprising therefore that *homo ferus*, reduced by circumstance to his bodily appetites,
takes a great interest in those who provide him with food once the
period of initial distrust is passed. There seems to be far less of a
biological basis for sexual drive. Many of the authors cited expressed
some surprise at their subjects' apparent lack of interest in sex.
Tomko was repelled by the slightest erotic suggestion, 'poor
Kaspar' displayed an extreme lack of passion and Peter of Hanover
lived to old age without ever having shown any sexual desires of any
kind. Only Victor, Kamala and the Kronstadt girl (after three years
of life in the company of humans) gave any indication that they
possessed sexual feelings. It hardly needs saying that their sense of
modesty grew as they readapted to society. Kaspar Hauser, for
example, would at first allow himself to be undressed and washed
without the slightest embarrassment, while later he became extremely shy and modest. Anselm von Feuerbach tells the story of
Spix and Martius's Brazilian girl who, after having lived unclothed
for years, could only be persuaded to pose naked for a Munich
painter under the threat of being returned to her natural state.

A close study has been made of feral man's perceptual faculties
and the results underline, among other things, the difficulty of
seeing in the light experienced by those who have spent much of
their life in the dark. According to Feuerbach, Kaspar found 'the
countryside in the full glory of summer' unbearable to look at, and
explained later that he had been overcome by the confused and

dazzling colours. On the darkest of nights, however, he could find his way about without any difficulty and took great delight in the gropings of his companions. Like Victor, on the other hand, he was unable to tell plane figures from reliefs, a pencil sketch, for instance, from a wood carving, and in general this made it difficult for him to distinguish the representation of an object from the object itself. Some of Sleeman's cases, the second Sekandra child and both Amala and Kamala were all able to see well in the dark. Together with this ability one should include remarkably acute hearing and a highly developed sense of smell. Jean de Liège, to cite just one case, could recognize his warden by smell from some distance, and almost all the others were said to sniff at objects in the way that cats and dogs do. There is much evidence also to suggest an almost complete insensitivity to changes in temperature. The Irish boy, Victor of Aveyron, one of Sleeman's cases, the Shajampur child and both the Midnapore girls all possessed this characteristic. The view that men outside society are not really men is lent yet more weight by the fact that peculiarly human traits like laughing and smiling are totally absent in wild children. Such emotions as they do display tend to be cruder and less specifically human. Tomko, Dina Sanichar, the Kronstadt child and Amala and Kamala all displayed anger and impatience.

The need for the company of those like oneself in their case took the form of a love of animals. Clemens, the pig-boy, befriended thick-skinned animals, Kaspar became completely absorbed when alone with horses and some of the Sleeman children were happy only in the company of dogs. Zingg remarks quite rightly that human desires develop only in the presence of the correct environmental stimuli, just as plants will develop only in the right soil with the right amount of light. He makes the equally pertinent suggestion that the best way of investigating the effects of society as a structure on man was to study wild children. These 'experiments with nature' provide confirmation for Jaspers's assertion in his *General Psycho-Pathology*: 'from the psychological point of view we become men by what we acquire through imitation and education'. The peculiarity of feral man's behaviour reveals how pointless it is to try to separate man's 'genetic programme' and the stages of his development from their particular realization in the process of learning. The inheritance of the species is once again shown to be nebulous indeed without a proper social apprenticeship.

II. AN ASSESSMENT AND INTERPRETATION
OF THE EVIDENCE

The evidence concerning wolf children has so far been presented without any consideration of its value. The time has now come for such an assessment. Total acceptance would be just as wrong as total rejection, and since doubts about its authenticity have been raised – some less well-intended than others – these must be answered.

A charge that is levelled at all the reports is their initial implausibility. Bousquet summarized the matter when he pointed out that survival in isolation is impossible for a child of less than three or four, and that isolation at a later age would never eradicate all traces of human culture. This dilemma, however, is less cruel than it seems. Many of the children who were abandoned very young – Amala, for instance – were protected by animals, while those isolated at a later stage in their lives were either arrested in their development or suffered a regression, like the sailor washed ashore on a desert island who on recovery was found to have lost his powers of speech, and whose story, incidentally, inspired Defoe to write a more optimistic version of the facts.

Let us examine the possibility of a regression taking place. There have indeed been cases of children 'adopted' by animals who have survived from a very young age but equally there have been cases of those who have enjoyed family life long enough to have learnt how to survive by themselves. It is more likely than not that such an unloving and distant upbringing was not an education at all but the first stage in the child's abandonment. It is absurd to insist as Bousquet did, and as Dennis has done more recently, that after four years of life a child must necessarily possess traces of civilization.[31] This does not, of course, answer their objection in the case of children abandoned by accident. Here too an explanation must be found for the child's loss of powers and his regression to an earlier stage of development.

Many authors stress the importance of reinforcement in the process of learning. The acquisition of a system of motor or mental abilities involves repetition and all acquired abilities disappear unless renewed by experience. Marian Smith suggests that the child's mental degeneration could be explained by the emotional trauma suffered on abandonment, replacing the theory of abandonment for backwardness with that of backwardness from isolation.[32] Arnold Gesell, however, had already rejected such an explanation as inadequate by pointing out that none of the best known cases displayed any of the usual symptoms of the main pathological syndromes: the dissociation found in schizophrenia, the compulsive behaviour of manic psychosis, or indeed the phantasies that accompany paranoia.[33] Even if Marian Smith were right it would only confirm the view that children – and adults too no doubt – deprived of human contact are reduced to a sub-human state without instincts to organize them. Whichever explanation is accepted – mental arrestation or emotional trauma – one avoids at least having to accept a third hypothesis, retained despite all the evidence, that the cause is from the beginning a defect of birth.

The ability of a child to survive without human company and not die of cold and hunger is still a matter for dispute. Dennis claims that children could rely on their own resources only for an extremely

31. Bousquet, op. cit., p. 43 above; W. Dennis, 'The Significance of Feral Man', *American Journal of Psychology*, 54, 1941, pp. 425–32. He argues that the behavioural characteristics of *homines feri* are to be explained by defects at birth and that survival in isolation can only last a very short time. See also Zingg's 'Reply to Professor Dennis' in *American Journal of Psychology*, 54, pp. 432–5. Dennis restates his position in 'A Further Analysis of Reports of Wild Children', *Child Development*, 22, 1951, pp. 153–8.

32. Marian Smith, 'Wild Children and the Principle of Reinforcement', *Child Development*, 25, 1954, pp. 115–23.

33. Arnold Gesell, *Wolf Child and Human Child* (Methuen, London 1941). He dismisses those who interpret as congenital deficiency backwardness caused solely by the lack of education.

short time, but this objection is really no more convincing than his previous one. There is a tendency to suspect evidence just because it is old or remote and yet at the same time there exists a readiness to accept a growing mass of stories that are 'stranger than fiction'. Why should one save one's incredulity for such natural enigmas as survival in the wild, and yet be quite prepared to believe the absurd stories which are offered daily in the press? One can leave the professional doubters to brood over this item which appeared recently in a Paris newspaper: 'A child who had fallen some hundred feet from the tenth floor of a block of flats was picked up with only a broken arm and said calmly: "Mimile went bump".' If Victor of Aveyron's good fortune strikes one as implausible what can one say when it comes to that of Mimile? It must be remembered of course that human nature was not called into question by Mimile's fall in quite the same way. In a world in which almost anything is to be expected and in which millions have survived the most intolerable conditions, it is not at all remarkable that there have been twenty, thirty or perhaps forty cases of extreme isolation. It would have been far more surprising if there had never been any at all. A 'wild' life is one possible mode of existence and, in the nature of things and by the law of numbers alone, cannot be ruled out as improbable. It is a far greater mistake to reject all the cases than to accept some of them. Again if one argues that *homines feri* can have lived in isolation only for a very short time, how is one to explain the hardening and thickening of the skin on the knees and elbows of the Midnapore sisters? How would one explain the unshakeable appetite for raw meat and offal displayed by all the wolf-children so far reported, or the dislike of meat of any kind shown by Victor? The theory that a 'wild' life can only last a short time conflicts, moreover, with the claims of local people in the Aveyron département that long before Victor's capture they had caught glimpses of him naked in the forest.

Another point of controversy is the incompatibility of animals and humans. Modern psychologists have conducted experiments which show that peaceful coexistence is possible between those 'hereditary' enemies kittens and mice and these should help us see that even the fiercest animals – wolves and bears for instance – could accept a human child in certain circumstances. After all, nobody doubts that sheep, pigs or cattle could tolerate the presence of a human child. That such different animals *have* cared for lost children is attested by the marked animal characteristics displayed by the Irish boy, the third Lithuanian child, the two Sekandra children or some of Sleeman's cases who used to sniff at their food like dogs. It would require some ingenuity to explain away why the second Sleeman child or the Midnapore girls drank by lapping water with their tongues, while the reluctance of the sceptics to draw the obvious conclusions from these children's eating habits, or from their refusal of clothing, can only be ascribed to professional caution.

Such persistence in the face of the evidence becomes extremely useful in the defence of lost causes. Bergen Evans's book *The Natural History of Nonsense* is an example of just this. An amusing but superficial writer, he questioned Zingg's sense of geography and criticized him for not knowing where Midnapore was. He also reproached the Reverend Singh for leaving out of the journal published in 1942 the evidence of the guides who accompanied him on his mission in 1920. But why should Bergen Evans (that scourge of journalists, in a style more journalistic than his victims) be more ready to trust the word of Singh's companions than Singh's own, especially since it is well known that the latter hesitated to publish his journal for so long because of his religious scruples? It is anyway slightly absurd to expect that these companions could be found after twenty years. Why should they be any easier to find in India than friends from some disbanded regiment in France or the United States? Bergen Evans's book is a thorough work in which certain traditional prejudices are combined with the author's own prejudiced conviction that people are more often wrong than right, and indeed he goes on to demonstrate this by a few mistakes of his own.[34]

The evidence, nevertheless, must be examined with care, especially when it comes from less dependable sources than Feuerbach, Singh or Itard. Many of the accounts we have mentioned are of doubtful

34. Bergen Evans, *The Natural History of Nonsense* (Michael Joseph, London 1947).

value and some of them are quite certainly inventions. One has only to cite the story told by one Sergeant Holsen, who claimed to have captured a small boy living among baboons on the coast near Bathurst in the Cape. The child had survived, he said, on a diet of uncooked wheat and cactuses. An investigation revealed that the boy, Lucas, was at the time of his alleged discovery nearly two hundred miles away in Burghersdorp. From here he was transferred to Grahamstown Mental Hospital where none of the staff, who looked after him throughout 1904, could remember any mention of his ever having lived among monkeys. Years later in 1931 a man named Muscott, but using the pseudonym of George Harvey Smith, revived the hoax and was signed for a film by a large Hollywood studio. However, the real Smith then decided to exhibit Lucas in London, and there turned out to be nothing extraordinary about him at all. His subnormality was quite obviously the result of an early skull fracture. Zingg included seven pages of 'evidence' in his 1940 article and put an end to this ridiculous story. He did not require a Bergen Evans to remind him of the need for caution when dealing with stories of *homines feri*.

One can have no serious doubts, however, about the lives of Kaspar of Nuremberg, Victor of Aveyron or Kamala of Midnapore. They are as dependable as any reliable historical record. As Anna Anastasi has put it: 'They help to clarify some of the findings about child development which have been established under more controlled conditions'.[35]

Here, as elsewhere, the value of the evidence must be assessed by confronting the witnesses in the manner of an examining magistrate. Jean Itard was a senior doctor at the Hospital for Deaf Mutes in Paris. Von Feuerbach was President of the Ansbach Court of Appeal and J. A. L. Singh was the rector of the Midnapore orphanage. A doctor, a lawyer and a priest: for whatever motive, their main interest was in the truth. Each gave painstakingly detailed accounts of *homo ferus* and there is not the slightest suggestion of collusion

---

35. Anna Anastasi, *Differential Psychology*, 3rd edn, Macmillan, New York 1962, pp. 107–12.

between them. Singh had read neither of the others and Feuerbach was unacquainted with Itard's work. Neither the judge nor the priest appeared to have studied Linnaeus, yet all three confirmed the two major characteristics singled out in his *Systema Naturae*: the difficulty which wild children experience in standing erect, and their initial muteness. Victor, admittedly, was an exception to the first, but his walk is described, somewhat ambiguously, as 'a trot and a gallop', and indeed Citizen Nougairolles, the Administrator of the Saint-Affrique Hospital, described him as running on all fours across a field when he realized he was on the point of capture. As regards the second characteristic, Victor never learnt to talk, Kamala's muteness grew less, and Kaspar made distinct progress towards speech. All three authors draw attention to the amorphousness of their charges' sexual instincts – which they could never have invented – and they noted the effect of isolation on their senses. Both Bonaterre and Von Feuerbach took special note that neither Victor nor Kaspar could recognize his reflection in the mirror. Any final hesitations must surely be overcome by considering the resemblance between these accounts, written as they were by careful and scrupulous men who could not possibly have communicated their results to each other.

It is not, however, to the evidence itself that 'philosophers of human nature' have directed their most serious criticisms so much as to its interpretation. Even Lévi-Strauss says that 'the majority of these children suffered from some congenital defect and their abandonment should therefore be treated as the consequence of the abnormality which almost all display and not, as often happens, as its cause'.[36] Note the careful reservations 'the majority' and 'almost all' by which Lévi-Strauss excludes the authentic cases we are dealing with here. It must be said that in his otherwise admirable work he deals with wolf children only in passing and has obviously not taken the time to acquaint himself fully with the literature. Almost all the references in the bibliography are mistaken either in title or date. He writes of one of the Midnapore children: 'He was unable

36. Lévi-Strauss, *The Elementary Structures of Kinship* (London 1968), p. 50.

to talk even as an adult.' This example is particularly ill-chosen because the child in question – a girl, by the way – learnt to speak quite fluently towards the end of her life, though with a limited vocabulary, and moreover never reached adulthood but died during adolescence at the age of seventeen. Arnold Gesell reckoned that if her progress had continued at the same rate she would by the time she was thirty-five have reached the mental age of a ten- or twelve-year-old, which is, as he points out, not so very different from that of a farm labourer in his own country – or ours for that matter.

Lévi-Strauss's theory is implicitly criticized by Merleau-Ponty in his discussion of an article by François Rostand which he cites with approval in *Les Relations avec autrui chez l'enfant*. The continued inability to speak cannot, he argues, be considered as conclusive evidence of constitutional backwardness:

There is a period during which a child is particularly sensitive to language and during which he can learn to talk. It has been shown that if the child ... is not in an environment in which there are people who talk then he will never be able to talk with the same ease as those who have learnt to speak during the period in question. This is what happens in the case of so-called wild children who have been brought up among animals or away from people who talked. These children never learn to talk with the same facility which ordinary children display ... (there is) a very close relationship between the acquisition of language and the child's family situation. ... Children suddenly and permanently separated from their mothers always suffer a linguistic regression. This is not only because the first word which a child speaks is 'mama' but because all language is, so to speak, maternal. ... The child's acquisition of language will take the same form as its relationship with its mother: one of identification. To learn to speak is to learn a series of roles, to adopt ways of behaving and linguistic gestures ... (using Piaget's expression). The child must learn to think reciprocally. ... The intellectual elaboration of our experience of the world is indissolubly linked to the elaboration of our inter-personal relations.[37]

To illustrate this view one has only to think of the tragic examples frequently provided in the press. There was a case reported in 1963 of Yves Cheneau from Saint-Brevin in Loire Atlantique who was

37. Maurice Merleau-Ponty, *'Les Relations avec autrui chez l'enfant'*, text of lecture given at the Collège de France (Centre de Documentation Universitaire, Paris, 1958) pp. 13–18.

discovered locked in a cellar by his uncle and the local police; he had been kept there for eighteen months by his step-mother. When he came out, his uncle said 'he took some time to readjust to the day-light. We showed him a cat and a cow and he was asked what they were. He had completely forgotten.' Didier Leroux, a special reporter from one of the large Paris dailies, saw him at the hospital in Nantes and wrote: 'His huge eyes slide sleepily over people and things. He did not speak. He has quite forgotten how.'

The theory that isolation must be the result of a family's refusal to accept the child's backwardness is founded, as we have shown, on a mistaken and retrospective interpretation of the child's dumbness. If one gives it a moment's thought one will realize just how untenable it is. What makes people think all or at least most cases of abandonment can be explained by the child's backwardness? Do social welfare statistics suggest that the majority of abandoned children suffer from some sort of idiocy or are subnormal in some way? Plenty of children are in fact abandoned simply because they are a hindrance or an embarrassment and not because of anything to do with their intelligence. All the evidence suggests that the same proportion of normal and subnormal children would be found among the cases of wolf children as would be found among those who appear in the lists of adoption agencies. To take a particular example, Amala, by the age of one and a half, had already spent many months in the forest and was deeply affected by her life there. It is highly unlikely that her callous and uncaring mother would have been able to detect any sign of future mental backwardness in such a newly-born baby. During periods of social upheaval, groups of orphaned or abandoned children wander the roads. They were a familiar sight during the Napoleonic wars, in Russia after the October Revolution, in Central Europe during the Second World War and in Italy in 1945. Thousands of Chinese Moses used to be sent floating down the Yangtse each year, bound for a certain death, while in India the chance sympathy of a wild animal has sometimes saved a child who would otherwise almost certainly have died. In none of these cases does the IQ of the stray have anything to do with the matter, any more than it has in the case of the abandoned nursling. Sometimes a mother is reluctant to separate herself completely from her child. We have already described the case of Yves Cheneau. There are also the cases of illegitimate children locked away whose life manages to be a sort of domestic wildness. Anna of Pennsylvania, for example, an illegitimate daughter born on 6 March 1932, was found in February 1938 shut away on the second storey of an isolated farm. She had at first been brought up by a nurse in a house for collective education where everyone agreed she was a normal – and rather pretty – child. But her mother was unable to pay the fees and took her away before she was more than a year old. She kept her in a darkened room, paid her no attention and gave her little food. After four years of confinement in one room – it seems that most of the time she had lain motionless on a dirty mattress – she displayed many of the characteristics of *homines feri*. She was unable to stand on her feet – a case of straightforward cachexia – and was incapable of making the slightest sound. She was in a state of pathological distraction, paying no attention to the toys she was given and never laughing or crying. She suffered various sensory incapacities and it was thought initially that she was both deaf and blind. As soon as her re-education began, she started to show preferences for certain foods and colours and developed a game with her nurse which involved them in placing their foreheads together. Physical examination revealed that her reflexes – knees, pupils, soles of feet – were all normal. She soon began to laugh loudly and happily and even to stand with some help. By the end of a year she was able to get down stairs alone by sitting on each step in turn, and could also feed herself. She learnt to drink out of a cup, to use a spoon, and with help to walk a few paces. After sixteen months she began to wash herself and showed some understanding of verbal instructions. Though nothing could make up for the time she had lost, her mental powers were nevertheless slowly awakened.

Another girl, Edith Riley, was kept in a wood shed for some years, and though she suffered less cruelly from her confinement and was less completely uprooted than Anna, she was classified at the age of twelve as a complete imbecile. Within two years she had reached a normal level of intelligence. In neither case was initial backwardness the original reason for confinement or rejection. Kingsley Davis, following Kellogg and F. S. Freeman, considers correctly that the mental deficiencies of wolf children are the consequences of their isolation from human society.[38] They point out that there is no reason for thinking that abandoned children include a larger proportion of congenital idiots than a representative sample of the population as a whole.

The argument that in most cases the reason for abandonment was severe cretinism can be defeated on another score. Arnold Gesell argues that the very ability to survive in such precarious conditions is itself a sign of normality. Neither imbeciles nor idiots, he says, could possibly survive without the help of other humans for more than a few days. Wild children retain mental faculties which continue to operate and which provide them with something more than what they already know. It is precisely this capacity for acquiring knowledge that enables them to draw a few feeble lessons from their experience and so maintain a rudimentary existence. Victor of Aveyron must have had a normal mental apparatus to have survived for so long by himself in the Rouergue woods. Gesell adds to this cogent argument another equally telling observation: Kamala, like Victor, quite clearly wanted to learn and to improve herself. She wanted to achieve maturity. These are clinical symptoms never found in natural idiots. They can never really communicate with their fellows and never progress beyond a mental age of about two. At the age of eight Kamala was backward only because of her external circumstances.

The accounts of wolf children must also be examined in the light of the clinical investigation of mentally deficient children. In both cases it is plausible to suppose that the lack of education or some family deficiency are the reasons for the children's psychological asphyxia and intellectual retardation. It is impossible to tell at first glance whether a particular case of mental backwardness is internally or externally caused. Gesell points out – and recent research supports him – that the careful observation of cases of extrinsic

38. See above, p. 47 n. 29.

backwardness – that is of backwardness which cannot be attributed to any organic defect – reveals a flicker of intelligence, a willingness to learn which is almost extinguished but which can be rekindled by patient teaching. On the basis of tests which measure learning ability, it is possible to distinguish physically-based mental deficiencies from those which arise from the peculiarities of the child's upbringing. These admittedly are no less severe and no less lasting, but they are nevertheless susceptible to psychiatric treatment.

One might well expect that a group of defectives in care would contain many more children with emotional problems than a reference group of backward children from a local school. At the first attempt, the number of failures in Penrose and Raven's *Progressive Matrices* test is the same for both groups. After four explanatory lessons, however, when the children are given the test again, those who are socially handicapped approach – although they do not reach – the level of normal children for the precise and limited problems they have to solve. On the other hand the children whose handicap is presumably organic in origin make only a marginal improvement in their scores. Hurtig, who conducted the experiment, shows that backwardness sometimes disguises quite straightforward social deprivations and that the capacity for improvement of one's score in this sort of test should be considered of diagnostic value. Returning to Gesell, the desire to learn and the capacity for improvement was for both Victor and Amala – not to mention Kaspar – evidence that their mental backwardness was not the result of some defect in their brains. At the age of twelve they had a mental age of two and from this point of view, they should have been classified as imbeciles. But their idiocy was not intrinsic. It was not, in other words, congenital or hereditary. They progressed slowly to a state which was still one of backwardness but in which they were able nevertheless to take some small part in social life, conduct rudimentary conversations and, in the case of Victor, even to read and write after a fashion.

But why do most wolf children reach their intellectual ceiling so soon – if one excludes Tomko and Kaspar who were never completely cut off from human company, and the Sogny girl who for a long time had a companion? The reason is that if social conditioning is to produce the right results it must occur at the right time. There is a particular age for talking, for walking, just as there is an age for reading, for algebra and Latin. Everything becomes abnormally difficult if for any reason whatsoever this stage is missed. To quote Gesell once more, wolf children have to unlearn what they have already acquired before they can begin learning once more. They have to wipe out every trace of their wolf-behaviour and skills. The progress they made was limited, but it *was* progress and it was wrong to conclude on the basis of their original behaviour what their future capacities would be. This is what Pinel did in the case of Victor and his judgement was proved to be wrong indeed. Their development, slow as it was, totally refuted the idea that mental backwardness was the original cause of their abandonment.

This debatable hypothesis might in fact prove correct in some cases where all attempts at education have failed. Zingg interprets the dullness of Dina Sanichar as proof *per contra* that it was the loss of human company which was responsible for the backwardness of Victor, Kaspar and Kamala. Tredgold described their condition, in a latinate jargon of his own, as *isolation amentia*,[39] a syndrome for which Rauber chose the more felicitous name of *dementia ex separatione*. Theirs are the three cases among wolf children which demonstrate the possibility of intellectual progress and emotional recovery. They deserve consideration in detail not only because they are all examples of the capacity for education but also because they illustrate so clearly the three main types of 'wildness': the child in confinement, the child among animals and the child in isolation.[40]

39. A. F. Tredgold, *Mental Deficiency* (New York 1920), p. 304.
40. Modern discussions of wolf children include: E. T. Kruger and W. C. Reckless, *Social Psychology* (Longmans, Green, New York 1931), pp. 38–9; G. M. Stratton, 'Jungle Children', *Psychological Bulletin*, 31, 1934, pp. 596–7; Kimball Young, *Sociology* (American Book Company, New York 1942), pp. 5–8, 11; F. C. Dockeray, *Psychology* (Prentice-Hall, New York 1942), pp. 82–3; E. D. Chapple and C. S. Coon, *Principles of Anthropology* (Holt, New York 1942), pp. 62–3; W. F. Ogburn, 'The Wild Boy of Agra', *American Journal of Sociology*, 64, 1959, pp. 449–54; Bruno Bettelheim, 'Feral Children and Autistic Children', *American Journal of Sociology*, 64, 1959, pp. 455–67.

3
The Major Examples
of the Three Main Types
# of Wolf Children

No one is insensible to hoaxes and indeed the majority of the cases considered belong in this category. The epidemic nature of their occurrence is striking: the year 1344 produced two cases in Germany, 1767 two in Hungary, and in the fifty-two years between 1843 and 1895 there were no less than fourteen wolf children reported in India. People called Singh were particularly gifted at finding them: one Singh came face to face with *homo ferus* in Batzipur, a second, according to Demaison, went all the way to Africa in order to justify his reputation by discovering Assicia, and Amala and Kamala were found by yet a third Singh. The story of Mademoiselle LeBlanc is filled with details more reminiscent of fairy tale than fact and even the accounts of Kaspar, Kamala and Victor contain large elements of fantasy.

All this might well deter historians, whatever their field, but it should not discourage us from seeking the kernel of truth in these accounts which many authors have wilfully disguised with the help of vivid imaginations. As we pointed out earlier in this introduction, so many ordinary events from the past baffle us that we should in no way be surprised if extraordinary happenings leave us guessing. I know various clever and well-established academics – not necessarily believers in human nature – who still dine out on stories about wolf children just as some still dine out on stories about the parish priest. They make cheap fun of them by exposing the absurdities and inconsistencies that can be found in many of the texts. Actually it is the content of the stories which really irritates them, for if they were to be consistent they would laugh at the whole mass of insignificant and contradictory documents which it is their job to rescue and put in some order. But let us ignore them and continue with this introduction to Itard's two reports by providing a simple and lucid account of the vital trio: Kaspar, Kamala and Victor.

At about five in the afternoon on 26 May 1828 an extraordinary young man tottered along Nuremberg's Unschlittplatz to the surprise of one of the citizens who was resting in a chair outside his house. This is how Anselm von Feuerbach begins the story of Kaspar in his book *Beispiel eines Verbrechens am Seelenleben des Menschen*.

This unknown boy was wearing a felt hat with a red leather band in which was stuck a faded picture of the city of Munich, a black silk scarf, faded jacket, coarse shirt, roughly made trousers and badly patched top-boots heeled not with leather but with horseshoes. His pockets contained a small handkerchief embroidered with his initials, some pieces of paper on which were scribbled a few Catholic prayers, a rosary and a small pack of gold dust. He was carrying a letter addressed to 'The Honourable Captain of the 4th Cavalry Squadron of the 6th Nuremberg Regiment', and so the astonished citizen took the boy to the local barracks where the mysterious letter was opened. It said in effect: 'This boy wishes to serve his king. He was entrusted to me by his mother. I have taught him to read and write, and brought him by night to Nuremberg.' On another sheet was written: 'The boy is baptized and his christian name is Kaspar. He was born on 30 April 1812. When he is seventeen, take him to Nuremberg where his father who is now dead served in the cavalry. I am only a poor girl.' The soldiers left Kaspar to sleep on the straw in the stables. They shook him awake at eight o'clock next morning and at about ten o'clock took him to the police station where he was given a pen and wrote his name: Kaspar Hauser.

At first Kaspar lived in a cell usually reserved for vagrants. He played with a coin and then with various toys which were brought to him by local people. Most of all he enjoyed playing with a horse, and this he adored. He had a man's body but the mind of a three-year-old child. He would do one thing only with his hands – pick up objects with his thumb and index finger. He slept from dusk to dawn and spent most of the day sitting on the ground with his legs stretched out in front of him. The warder, Hietel, said that he would sometimes play with the local children. Kaspar walked like a drifting boat, moving slowly forward with hesitant steps and then swinging suddenly backwards. He would not eat meat and used to spit out beer because it gave him fevers, headaches and all sorts of pains. He preferred bread and water. He cried frequently, shouted out and was frightened by everything and nothing. He laughed when he was happy, particularly when he saw white horses, though black ones terrified him. When there was nothing to distract him, he lapsed into a sort of brutish passivity. He amused himself by writing the letters of the alphabet, the numbers from one to ten, and by covering whole pages with his signature. He could scarcely be said to speak at all and was only able to utter a jumble of sounds and the odd sentence or word in patois: *ä fechtene möcht ih wähn wie mei wottä wähn is* (I want to be a soldier like my father), *hoam weissa* (*heim weiss er*: he knows the way home), and *woas nit* (*weiss nicht*: I don't know), *bua* for anything human and finally *ross* (horse), one of the six words he knew, for anything animal. 'He could have been taken for a creature from another planet who had landed miraculously on earth,' wrote Feuerbach after he had visited him on 11 July, 'or for the man in Plato who had been brought up underground and had never seen the sun until he was grown-up.' On 18 July 1828 Kaspar left the police station for the house of Dr Daumer who had taken pity on him. After a few months his face began to acquire a certain symmetry and he lost his very noticeable prognathism. He was a thick-set boy with clear blue eyes, fine skin and delicate hands. He had a number of scars from recent cuts and a fairly deep wound on his right arm. He complained of violent headaches and drank quantities of water.

Within a few weeks he had learnt how to climb the stairs and his new guardian had persuaded him to eat meat. By September he was strong enough to lift a weight of twelve kilos with both hands. In his cell Kaspar had offered his toy horses his own food, garlanded them with bits of paper and put them carefully away in their box at night time, displaying in all this an abnormal mania for tidiness. Once settled at Daumer's, he played less and began to draw instead. He took days over an attempt to copy a lithograph, making nearly a hundred sketches, the last few of which began to resemble the original. A certain Von Rumpler taught him how to mount a horse and this gave him indescribable pleasure. Gradually his steps became less hesitant and his emotions more stable. He got used to sleeping in a bed but remained terrified of anything unfamiliar to him. He would become almost paralysed by new things and by certain colours, especially black, green (which might explain his dislike of the countryside) and yellow (except for the shiny gold of his coins). He disliked all smells except for those of bread, aniseed and cummin. The presence of magnetized metals made him feel ill but in December this curious weakness suddenly disappeared.

Kaspar was completely docile, his only complaint being that he had been abandoned. He realized that he was different and wondered why he had no parents. He preferred girls' clothes to boys' because they were prettier and objected strongly when told that he had to become a man. Somewhat later he grew to accept the idea of marriage and the presence in the house of a female companion, but he could conceive of such a person only as a housekeeper and the idea of love between man and woman never entered his head. According to Daumer, Kaspar was at first unable to judge distances and had no sense of perspective. Though he could not stand the sunlight, he was able to see perfectly well in the dark. He could not grasp the idea of his reflection and whenever he was placed in front of a mirror he would always look behind it to see who it was looking at him. In the stories he told, he confused dreams with reality. His hearing was extremely keen but he was curiously insensitive to the sound of a ticking clock or to church bells. During military parades he liked to get as near as possible to the bass drum though the crowds disturbed him. When he watched the riding from his window however, just the opposite occurred and he became quite terrified by the sound of music.

Kaspar had to be educated, or rather re-educated, from the very beginning. As soon as he went to live with Daumer, he began to learn to speak. He learnt infinitives to start with, used semantemes rather than morphemes and spoke of himself in the third person. He acquired the use of 'I' only very slowly. He did not understand the use of imperative or subjunctive forms and his speech was scattered with curious polysemes: he used the word *berg* (mountain), for instance, to describe anything tall. He did not speak in well-defined sentences but in clauses which followed each other without clear grammatical connections.

All of this was to change in the next three years. Each morning between eleven and twelve Kaspar went for an arithmetic lesson in the town, and was made to learn Latin at the local school. In 1831 he spent a few weeks with Feuerbach who was dismayed at the conventional education being forced on so abnormal a young man. His powers of concentration in the classroom were not strong and he soon became taciturn and bad-tempered. Though slow-witted, he was always full of simple and direct questions: 'Who made the trees?' 'Who puts out the stars and lights them up?' 'Where is my soul?' 'Can I look at it?' 'Why doesn't God answer my prayers?' Kaspar's memory was of little help in telling who he was or where he had come from. He sought desperately to remember and a few details came back from the past. He seemed to think he had 'arrived in the world' and 'discovered men' in Nuremberg. Before this, he had lived in 'a hole' or 'a cage' on a diet of bread and water. He had once been put to sleep with some opium, the smell of which he recognized at Daumer's house, and he remembered playing with two wooden horses during his imprisonment. His daily food had been brought to him by someone whom he never saw and who would sometimes stand behind him drawing figures, letters and numbers over his shoulder. This was the first person he could remember and he referred to him simply as 'Man'. It was soon reported in the town that Kaspar was about to reveal his secret. The excited gossip which ensued was to prove fatal, for on 17 October 1829 he had a visit from someone who must have been 'The Man'. Kaspar was ill at the time and alone in the house with Daumer's mother-in-law and his sister Katharina. Around midnight Katharina discovered some drops of blood on the stairs and in the hall. She looked for Kaspar everywhere and could not find him. He was finally discovered in the cellar half-dead; all he could say was 'Man' over and over again. He had been badly wounded on the temple, spent the next forty-eight hours in a dangerous coma, and took almost a month to recover fully. It turned out that 'The Man' had been seen in the town and recognized. Feuerbach's cryptic comment, that he was 'not allowed to reveal' all he knew, no doubt added to the heated curiosity of those who were following the story and eagerly awaiting some further revelation. One day in 1833, while staying with Feuerbach, when he was just twenty-two, Kaspar was attacked for a second time in the park at Ansbach. He was stabbed with a knife and died the following day. A small monument was later erected on the spot where he had fallen inscribed with the words: 'Here one unknown was murdered by another.' This has turned out to be only half-true. It is almost certain that Kaspar was in fact the son of Stéphanie Beauharnais, Joséphine's niece, who had been married off by Napoleon to Prince Charles of Baden. So that the crown would revert to the children of a morganatic line, Kaspar, the son of Charles and Stéphanie, was taken away from them and entrusted to the care of Baron Griesenberg's game-keeper, Franz Richter, otherwise known as 'The Man'. The name of his murderer was Johann Jacob Muller. These revelations were made only sometime afterwards by Edmond Bapst, who threw light on what was indeed a mysterious and murky business.

Kaspar Hauser figures in the literature of isolation as the child not totally deprived of the company of others but who lived alone in the silence and darkness of his cell. The experience of children who have lived with animals all their lives is completely different.

In his book *Wolf Child and Human Child*, Arnold Gesell gives a striking account, based on the original source material, of the misfortunes of Amala and Kamala, the two best known cases of zoanthropy.

On 9 October 1920 the Reverend Singh, who was preaching in the area, was told by the villagers of Godamuri that there were 'fantastic people' living in the forest. He was taken to the place under cover of dusk and saw some wolves emerging from their lair. There were three adults, two cubs and two 'monsters', one much smaller than the other, whose faces were hidden by their tangled hair and who were walking on all fours. Both of them behaved exactly like the wolves. As they came out of their cave, they put their heads out first and looked around before leaping out. Singh only just managed to prevent one of his guides from shooting and because they were all so terrified by the 'monsters', he went to another village seven miles away to recruit volunteers who had not yet heard of these strange creatures. When his party returned to the place a week later, two of the elder wolves fled, but the third, a she-wolf, stayed guarding the entrance to the cave, and was riddled with arrows. At the back of the cave they found two cubs and two children huddled together, the latter cowering in defence, the former ready to attack. The two Mowglis were entrusted to the villagers for a week but as soon as Singh left, they ran away from the children and on his return he found them abandoned in their enclosure almost dead from starvation. They were forced to drink milk and generally attended to, and after a few days Singh took them in an ox-cart to the orphanage which he ran in Midnapore, arriving there on 4 November 1920.

The younger one was given the name of Amala and the older one Kamala. Kamala had large shoulders, long arms and her spine was quite straight. With both of them, the skin on their hands, knees and elbows was heavily calloused. Their tongues hung out through thick red lips, they panted and frequently bared their teeth. They suffered from photophobia and day-blindness, and spent their days crouched in the shade or standing motionless with their faces to the wall. They livened up at night, howling and groaning and hoping to escape. Amala – aged one and a half – and Kamala – aged eight and a half – slept only about four hours in twenty-four. They had two means of getting about: on their knees and elbows for short distances and on their hands and feet for longer distances or for running. They lapped up liquids and took their food in a crouching position. Their exclusive taste for meat led them to indulge in the only activity of which they were capable: chasing chickens or rooting around for carcasses and entrails. Though they took a slight interest in dogs and cats, they were completely unsociable and used to snarl at humans, showing particular hostility to Singh's wife. When anyone approached, they used to arch their backs menacingly and shake their heads rapidly back and forwards to show their wariness.

Amala died on 21 September 1921 from nephritis and generalized oedema after an illness which had lasted three weeks, and curiously enough Kamala died of the same disease eight years later on 14 November 1929. The Reverend Singh and Dr Sarbadhicari kept a careful record of Kamala's psychological development throughout her stay at the orphanage. Singh's journal shows that her movements became slowly more human and that after ten months she was able to reach out her hand to take food. By February 1922 she was able to kneel and by March she could walk on her knees. In May she got to her feet leaning against a bench and the next summer stood up by herself for the first time. She had learnt to walk by January 1926 and for the remaining two years of her life, though her walk remained somewhat wolf-like, she showed quite clearly that her previous way of walking had been due merely to the absence of ordinary human training. Kamala's behaviour became year by year more relaxed and more varied. Endlessly repeated motor gestures, like pulling on the rope of a punkah for hours at a time, slowly gave way to actions of a social nature such as using a glass to drink from, chasing the crows which were eating grain in the farmyard, washing and bathing in front of the Singhs, looking after the smaller children at the orphanage and telling the nurses when they were crying, collecting eggs from the henhouse and many other simple tasks.

At the same time, her character was changing, though her sister Amala's death caused a temporary regression. She cried for the first time, refused all food or drink for two days, sat crouched in the corner for a week, and continued sniffing around for her companion's scent for a further four days. After three terms at the orphanage she became more confident and would take biscuits from Mrs Singh and even approach her at milk-time. Exactly as Itard had done, Mrs Singh began to massage the child's muscles in order to loosen them and unstiffen her joints. One day in November 1921 she took Mrs Singh's hand and showed by gestures that she wanted to be stroked. During the same month she sat down beside two kid goats, hugged them, and spoke to them in some incomprehensible language of her own. It was three years before she began to show fear of the dark and to want to sleep near the other children. She worried whenever Mrs Singh was not with her and would wander around the garden, greeting her return by leaping for joy and rushing to meet her. Over a period of five years, her sense of taste became gradually more discriminating and her emotional responses in general less crude. She developed a liking for salt and by 1926 had given up eating carrion. She avoided dogs, cried when the other children went to market without her and was impatient for her turn on the swing. She enjoyed compliments of any sort and showed her modesty by refusing to leave the dormitory without her dress on.

Kamala's intelligence also slowly improved. To begin with she knew only two words: '*ma*' for 'mama', meaning Mrs Singh, and '*bhoo*' which she used as an expression of hunger or thirst. By 1923 she could signal 'yes' or 'no' by nodding her head and say 'yes' ('*hoo*') in words. In 1924 she asked for rice with the word '*bha*' and showed her will for the first time by using the words '*am jab*' (I want). By 1926 Kamala could recognize her own cup and plate and was capable of carrying on a rudimentary conversation with a vocabulary of about three dozen words. She could understand verbal instructions and whenever she did not know a word she used sign language instead. Towards the end of her life in 1929 she had acquired the use of about fifty words and was able to talk quite easily with the doctors who looked after her, and call them by name. Paul Sivadon is correct in pointing out that there is no evidence at all that Kamala's backwardness was the consequence of some innate defect.[1] A comparison of her mental faculties as they were when she was eight years old with her faculties at the end of her life shows that her pitiable condition was due only to the lack of a proper family so early in life. In citing the story of Kamala, Sivadon reminds one that 'organic defects and psychological problems cannot be separated' and he concludes:

Man differs from animals in that he is born prematurely. His personality develops within a system of cultural matrices which are as important as the maternal matrix. They consist of emotional ties which are built up during the first two years of life with the mother and which affect the child's whole emotional life. Learning to speak at the correct time similarly makes all the difference to the child's intellectual life. This means that a child which is perfectly normal at birth can develop into an idiot if his education is unfavourable enough. It is extremely important to grasp this. The personality develops in exact proportion as the educative value of the environment offers the correct cultural support at the right moment.

On this subject Sivadon, a psychiatrist, shares the views of Merleau-Ponty, a psychologist and philosopher.

Amala and Kamala lived among wolves and so like Kaspar were never completely isolated. The most radical isolation seems to have been Victor's. In 1797 a naked child was seen playing entirely alone in the woods of Lacaune in the département of Tarn. He was captured for the first time in a place called La Bassine but escaped for a further fifteen months. In July 1798 he was spotted in a tree by some hunters, captured once again and taken to the house of a

1. Paul Sivadon, 'Infirmes et Incurables', in *Recherches Universitaires*, March–April 1963, p. 21, cited in *Esprit*, November 1965, pp. 636–7. A culturist interpretation of Kamala's backwardness by the Professor of Psychiatry at the Faculty of Medicine in Brussels.

widow in the village nearby. There he stayed for a week but managed to get away once more and according to Guiraud, a local government official, spent the long winter months in the woods. On 9 January 1800 at seven in the morning he strayed on to the road and was recaptured eight hundred metres from the village in the garden of a man named Vidal, a dyer from the district of Saint-Sernin-sur-Rance in the département of Aveyron. On 10 January Victor was placed in the hospital at Saint-Affrique and on 4 February he was taken to Rodez where he was given his first examination by the naturalist Bonaterre who also wrote the first report about him.[2]

The boy was about four and a half feet tall and his knee ligaments were normal. He murmured while he ate, was subject to sudden fits of anger, liked fires, slept according to the sun, tried constantly to escape and could not understand his reflection in the mirror – he always looked for the person he was sure was hiding behind the glass. The newspapers carried various stories about him and a government minister became interested in his case. Victor was taken to Paris for further studies and examined by Pinel, the most celebrated psychologist of the day. He reported that far from being a normal child deprived of all faculties by his extraordinary experiences, Victor was rather a congenital idiot exactly like the many others in the Bicêtre asylum. Itard, recently appointed consultant to the Institution des Sourds-Muets in the Rue Saint-Jacques, took the opposite view. He had read Locke and Condillac and was convinced that man is not 'born' but 'constructed'. He agreed the child was an idiot but denied that this was necessarily due to a defect of birth, arguing that it might equally well be explained by his cultural loss. He hoped to disprove his opponents by awakening the boy's mind. Victor was accordingly entrusted to his care so that he might have the opportunity of demonstrating his theory.

When he first arrived at the Institute, the boy's face twitched nervously, he kept rubbing his eyes, gnashing his teeth and jumping up and down. He suffered convulsions and made constant attempts

2. Bonnaterre, *Notice Historique* . . . , op. cit., p. 42 above.

to run away. His mood swung erratically from nervous excitement to complete passivity. He loved playing in the snow and enjoyed gazing Narcissus-like into the still waters of the pond. At night he would stare long and admiringly at the moon. He was incapable of imitation and showed not the slightest interest in the other children's games, although he enjoyed setting fire to some ninepins that someone gave him. The only work he could do, and this he must have learnt at Rodez or in the wilds, was shelling beans.

The doctor was struck that, at the age of puberty, his attempts at sexual satisfaction were absolutely futile, and that he did not seem to notice sexual differences. Itard was equally struck by some of the boy's other traits. His skin, though delicate, seemed insensitive to pain: he would readily pick burning logs out of the fire. He could not smell snuff even when it was put up his nose, and paid no attention to the noise of a gun fired right behind him, although he would turn at the sound of a nut being cracked. He disliked sleeping in a bed and was able to tolerate intense cold and damp. Foul smells did not trouble him at all. He ate berries, roots and raw chestnuts and disliked sweet things, spices, spirits and wines. He loved the rain and the storm clouds which announced its coming. In short, Victor scorned the products of civilization and preferred his nature plain and simple.

His powers of concentration were very poor and the slightest movement was sufficient to distract him. He was incapable of distinguishing a picture from the object it depicted and seemed not to hear music or the sound of the human voice, though he recognized at once the sound of a chestnut being shelled. He used to sniff at everything he came across, whether it was branches and leaves, stones, soil, or flesh. He was more helpless than a chimpanzee and could neither open a door by himself nor climb on to a chair to reach what he wanted. He was as incapable of speech as an animal and uttered only a single, formless sound. Victor's backwardness was revealed unmistakably in his face. His expression would change rapidly from a sullen scowl to a curious sneer, a muscular contortion meant to be a smile.

In the next few years Itard set about trying to effect some changes in the boy. He wrote two reports, published in 1801 and 1806 respectively, and described how, first after one year and then after six, the boy had lost some of his wildness. In the first account Itard tells how Victor stopped wetting his bed and learnt to dress himself; he now laid the table, held out his plate to be served, and filled up the water jug when it was empty. When he got bored with visitors, he would escort them firmly to the door, and often got sightseers to take him around the yard in a small wheelbarrow. When Itard deliberately ruffled his hair to see what he would do, he brought the doctor his comb, and he laid out his nurse's toilet things in the morning if he was in a hurry for his walk.

His sensibility became gradually more refined and his emotional life noticeably richer. He learnt to appreciate different temperatures by taking hot baths and showers and managed to recognize the idea of comfort and well-being. He refused to eat potatoes unless they were properly cooked and his sense of smell developed as he went down with his first cold. He still enjoyed a few of the old pleasures like watching a trickle of water fall on to his hand, gazing at things floating in a pool and following the play of light on the ceiling. His desire for escape returned whenever he saw the country again although he had grown very attached to Madame Guérin, his gouvernante, to Lemeri, the caretaker of the Observatoire garden, and to Itard himself, except when an extra-long 'lesson' sent him into a rage. His intellectual interests remained limited, although his powers of concentration became somewhat stronger. He learnt to follow with his eye the movements of a small object hidden under different cups. He was still totally unresponsive to all phonetic sounds except the vowel 'o' and it was for this reason that Itard chose for him the name 'Victor'.

He gradually learnt to pronounce all the vowels except 'u' and three consonants, among them 'l' which was the initial letter of his first word: '*lait*'. He did not use the word to ask for milk but said it when milk was offered to him as a sort of exclamation of pleasure. Itard was determined to teach him to speak and devised for this purpose a whole lot of boards with pictures on them so that Victor could cover each one with the appropriate object, starting off with everyday objects, and progressing to geometrical shapes, finally using the letters of the alphabet. Itard then moved from the individual letters to whole words (here at least he remained a traditionalist), and it was in this way that Victor learnt the word *lait*. He could recognize it in its written form as well as speak it and could make the word with letters and offer it when he wanted to ask for milk.

Itard's second report in 1806 describes Victor's further progress, though even after six years he was still rough and awkward. His one great invention, conceived in a rare flash of creativity, was a pencil-holder which he made from a skewer. Most of his time he spent in simple routine tasks like chopping wood, and he seemed to enjoy watching the logs split and drop on to the stones of the yard. He liked making himself useful and took particular pleasure in laying the table very carefully; it was his care for this task that led to a moving episode after Madame Guérin's husband had died. Victor laid his place as usual and when Madame Guérin came into the room and saw it she burst into tears. Victor, visibly upset, realized his mistake, cleared the place away and never laid it again.

Itard tells the story of Victor's slow socialization and the radical changes which he experienced in his emotional attitudes. After three years at the Rue Saint-Jacques he still regretted his lost freedom and longed for the forests. At a gathering in Clichy-la-Garenne, attended by Madame de Staël and other celebrities, Victor gave a demonstration of his tree-climbing skill.[3] When Itard took him to dine in town he had to be taken by cab, otherwise Victor would run on ahead. Whenever he could not go out for his usual walk, he became miserable and tried to run away from the Institute. Sometimes he managed to get as far as Denfert in the south of Paris or to the Senlis wood in the north, but he always felt sorry for it afterwards. After one such escape, he was caught by the police and kept in prison for two weeks until he was identified; he fainted

3. This episode is described in Edouard Herriot, *Madame Recamier et ses Amis* (Payot, Paris 1924), pp. 75–6.

from excitement on seeing Madame Guérin again. He was anxious to please his teachers, to understand and to learn. He laughed when Itard praised him, cried when he was rebuked and seemed more responsive to moral than to physical sanctions. He accepted punishments when he thought them justified, but objected when they were arbitrary or intended merely as experiments.

Under Itard's tutelage his intellectual faculties showed a remarkable development, despite the occasional harshness which his teacher employed. Itard had noticed that Victor was very much afraid of heights and one day when he refused to work at his lessons Itard took him up to the fourth storey and held him out of the window. Within a couple of minutes a pale and terrified Victor was ready for his lessons and for the first time began to cry.

Itard was a thoroughgoing follower of Condillac and considered that the education of the senses was of primary importance. He taught Victor to use his finger-tips to distinguish hot and cold chestnuts at the bottom of a bag, to tell chestnuts from acorns, and nuts from pebbles by their shape and feel, as well as cut-out letters of the alphabet. He taught him also to distinguish the sound of a bell from a drum, and a stick beaten against metal and against wood. Victor could also identify various letters and by the end of his first year he could recognize a few words and use them to ask for things, though he could not speak. Itard tried to take things a step further. He wrote words on a blackboard and made Victor follow their line with his finger to get him used to their shape and spelling. He then placed the objects which the words stood for beside the words and let Victor connect the two. He finally removed the objects and, pointing to each word in turn, got Victor to select the appropriate object.

Victor struggled for a long time with the problem of grasping and expanding concepts. At first the word 'book' meant only his teacher's bedside book – one particular object. Later, just as very young children do, Victor made the opposite mistake of using the word to describe anything remotely similar – a newspaper, a notebook, or an exercise book. After many lessons he began to achieve the right balance, using words correctly to catch the resemblance and difference between things. Itard taught Victor to label not only objects, but relationships between them, such as differences in size, and he also taught him to respond to words describing actions. This method of teaching was intended from the start to enable Victor to involve himself and participate properly in the act of learning. He remained unable to talk but very slowly learnt to write. The doctor made him copy simple figures, trace patterns with a stick, and follow the contours of written words with a pencil. By the end of several months it was clear that Victor had lost the status of idiot for ever. He was able to understand the meaning of words, and could express the simplest of his needs and wishes in writing.

On 3 May 1806, Itard received a letter from the Ministry of the Interior informing him that the government would continue to pay the 150 francs allocated to 'the good Madame Guérin' for her 'care and attention' in looking after the 'wild boy from Aveyron', and when Victor was eighteen Itard entrusted him entirely to the care of this lady. Victor went to live in an annexe of the Institute at 4 Impasse des Feuilliantines and stayed there until his death at the age of forty in 1828.

This is not the place to discuss Victor's place in the study of wolf children since this has already been touched on earlier. It would instead be valuable to comment on the opposition which Itard encountered from those who maintained the essentialist prejudices of the time. It must be remembered that, compared with the present, psychological 'knowledge' then occupied the same place in the sciences of man as alchemy had once occupied in the natural sciences. At the beginning of the nineteenth century it was generally believed that human infants, with the rare exception of those with physical defects, were miniature adults already fully equipped for life. Bousquet, for instance, seized triumphantly on Victor's obvious backwardness and the slowness of his improvement as confirmation of this theory.[4] He wrote:

If it was really only the lack of example which prevented him from breaking the restraints on his mind, then nothing should have prevented him from developing his powers to the full once he had breathed the air of civilization.

4. A. Bousquet, 'Eloge Historique d'Itard', in *Memoires de l'Académie de Médicine* (Paris 1840), vol. 8, pp. 1ff. Republished in Bourneville, op. cit., pp. 11–28. In this

Nothing, that is, except the impossibility of being six years old again, of miraculously curing his intellectual sclerosis, or effacing the trauma of his long unhappy years in isolation. Bousquet spoke as if the past counted for nothing, as if childhood played no role in the development of the adolescent or the life of the adult, as if mental backwardness could be made to vanish magically with a glance or a word. One is inevitably reminded in this context of racists or theorists of the right who are ready to accept differences in the conditions of life of different people, yet who try to justify their existence (usually hypocritically and always fallaciously) by pointing to their consequences. Esquirol, a contemporary of Itard, used precisely this fallacy in treating Victor as 'a native idiot who ran away from home or who was abandoned by his heartless parents'. Delasiauve and Bourneville argued even less persuasively. The first said straight out that Itard's savage was 'what his nature destined him to be', and the second did not bother to contradict him. Both felt that Itard's pedagogical experiments would have been more successful if they had been less 'sparing and abstract' and based instead on a 'coherent and above all practical approach' which would have 'encouraged rivalry, a stimulant to both idiots and normal children'. He is right, one must admit, that if Itard had proceeded in this way the result might have been 'more polished'.[5]

---

lecture, given on 1 December 1839, Bousquet cited Itard's year of birth mistakenly as 1775. The baptismal register for Oraison, kept at the town hall, gives the correct date of 25 April 1774.

Nineteenth-century discussions of wolf children concentrated on the question posed by F. J. Gall and G. Spurzheim: 'whether or not these children, deprived of all education, had not been imbeciles to begin with': *Anatomie et Physiologie du Système Nerveux en général et du Cerveau en particulier* (Paris 1810), p. 42. Among the other works in which the debate may be followed are: J. F. Blumenbach, *Beiträge zür Naturgeschichte* (Göttingen 1811) a statement of the 'biologistic' case; English translation: *The Anthropological Treatises of Johann Friedrich Blumenbach* by Thomas Bendyshe (Longmans, London 1865); Karl Rudolphi, *Grundriss der Physiologie* (Berlin 1821), vol. 1, pp. 25–6; J. F. I. Tafel, *Die Fundamentale Philosophie in genetischer Entwicklung mit Rücksicht auf die Geschichte jedes einzelnen Probleme* (1848), vol. 1, p. 44; Tafel presents the argument that the backwardness of wild children is due to their isolation. Tylor (op. cit., 1863) and Rauber (op. cit., 1885) both attacked Blumenbach from a culturalist standpoint.

5. Delasiauve, in Bourneville, op. cit., pp. 29–47.

Bourneville took the matter a step further, and suggested that the habits acquired in the forest were an obstacle to his education:

One of the main reasons why Itard's efforts, despite his ingenuity and intelligence, were not more fruitful was undoubtedly the age of his pupil. . . . The boy had to struggle not only against the cerebral damage which [could have] arrested the development of his mental faculties but also against the habits which he had acquired in the wild.[6]

The only thing wrong with this statement is that it implies that his retardation was both innate and acquired. It is almost certain that Victor spent several years in the mountainous forests of Languedoc and Rouergue, yet his autopsy revealed no sign of the alleged brain damage. The argument that Victor's backwardness was due to organic causes is like so many other unwarranted assumptions about the boy. They are an escape from the fact that his innate idiocy cannot be proved. There is no reason to suggest that he suffered from some defect at birth and indeed all the evidence points to the contrary.

Itard was occasionally unsettled by the attacks of his colleagues. He was himself to some extent a prisoner of the ideology of his time, tending to relate his teaching programme too closely to his psychological diagnosis. Yet nothing could shake his Condillacian interpretation of the facts. In 1806 he spoke with bitterness and contempt of those who had lost interest in the child because they had written him off as hopeless. He refused to allow himself the easy solution of convenient theories which he could not accept with all sincerity or let himself be trapped by easy sophistry. He stressed repeatedly Victor's progress in perception and his use of the main intellectual faculties and went on to emphasize his ability to understand signs, his growing self-control, the development in the boy of moral scruples and his acquisition of a sense of guilt.

The Members of the Institute who read Itard's second report agreed almost word for word with his conclusion. As a colleague, Dacier wrote: 'On the matter of Victor, one must consider what he was like at the beginning and what progress he has made, for to

6. Bourneville, ibid.

be judged fairly he can only be compared with himself.' After six years of observation and experiment Itard remained faithful to the view which he expressed so elegantly in the first report:

Cast on this globe, without physical powers, and without innate ideas; . . . In the savage horde the most vagabond, as in the most civilised nations of Europe, man is only what he is made to be by his external circumstances . . . he enjoys, from the enviable prerogative of his species, a capacity of developing his understanding by the power of imitation, and the influence of society (p. 91 below).

But he cannot achieve this on his own. The lessons and examples which he requires are provided only by his human surroundings and by the magic of his relationships with others. Itard was right that, without education, there is scarcely the possibility of man, let alone the promise.

LIST OF RECORDED CASES

	Description	Date of Discovery	Age at Discovery (in years)	First Detailed Report
1	The Hesse wolf-child	1344	7	Camerarius 1702 Rousseau 1754 Linnaeus 1758
2	The Wetteravian wolf-child	1344	12	Von Schreber 1775
3	The first Lithuanian bear-child	1661	12	Linnaeus 1758
4	The Irish sheep-child	1672	16	Tulp 1672 Linnaeus 1758
5	The Bamberg calf-child	about 1680		Camerarius 1702 Linnaeus 1788
6	The second Lithuanian bear-child	1694	10	Condillac 1746 Rousseau 1754
7	The third Lithuanian bear-child		12	Connor 1698

	Description	Date of Discovery	Age at Discovery (in years)	First Detailed Report
8	The Kranenburg girl (Holland)	1717	19	Linnaeus 1788
9–10	The two boys of the Pyrenees	1719		Rousseau 1754 Linnaeus 1758
11	Peter, the wild boy of Hanover	1724	13	Rousseau 1754 Linnaeus 1758
12	The Sogny girl (Champagne)	1731	10	Louis Raçine 1747 La Condamine 1755 Linnaeus 1788
13	Jean de Liège		21	Digby 1644 Linnaeus 1758
14	Tomko of Zips (Hungary)	1767		Wagner 1794
15	The Karpfen bear-girl (Hungary)	1767	18	Bonnaterre 1800
16	Victor, the wild child of Aveyron	1799	11	Itard 1801
17	Kaspar Hauser of Nuremberg	1828	17	Von Feuerbach 1832
18	The Salzburg sow-girl		22	Horn 1831
19	The Husanpur child	1843		Sleeman 1858
20	The first Sultanpur child	1843		Sleeman 1858
21	The second Sultanpur child	1848		Sleeman 1858
22	The Chupra child	1849		Sleeman 1858
23	The first Lucknow child			Sleeman 1858
24	The Bankipur child			Sleeman 1858
25	Captain Egerton's child			Sleeman 1858
26	Clemens, the Overdyke pig-child			Tylor 1863
27	The Overdyke wolf-child			Tylor 1863
28	Dina Sanichar of Sekandra	1872	6	Ball 1880
29	The second Sekandra child	1874	10	Ball 1880

	Description	Date of Discovery	Age at Discovery (in years)	First Detailed Report
30	The Shajampur child	towards 1898	6	Ball 1880
31	The second Lucknow child	1876		Ball 1880
32	The Jalpaiguri girl	1892	8	*Journal of the Anthropological Society of Bombay*
33	The Batzipur child	1893	14	Frazer 1929
34	The Kronstadt wolf-child		23	Rauber 1885
35	The Justedal snow-hen		12	Le Roux 1895
36	The Sultanpur child	1895	4	Ross 1895
37	Lucas, the South African baboon-child	1904		Foley 1940
38	The Indian panther-child	1920		Demaison 1953
39	Amala of Midnapore	1920	2	Squires 1927
40	Kamala of Midnapore	1920	8	Squires 1927
41	The first leopard-child			Stuart Baker 1920
42	The Maïwana child			*The Pioneer*, 5 April 1927
43	The Jhansi child	1933		Zingg 1940
44	An Indian wolf-child			Hutton 1939
45	The Casamance child	1930s	16	Demaison 1953
46	Assicia of Liberia	1930s		Demaison 1953
47	The second leopard-child		8	Zingg 1940
48	Anna of Pennsylvania	1938	6	Davis 1940
49	Edith of Ohio	1940		Maxfield 1940
50	The Syrian gazelle-child	1946		Demaison 1953
51	Ramu, the New Delhi child	1954	12	Agence France Presse 8 February 1954
52	The Mauritanian gazelle-child	22 Sept. 1960		Auger, April 1963
53	The Teheran ape-child	1961	14	Agence France Presse 28 Sept. 1961

A Note
on Jean Itard

Jean Marc Gaspard Itard was born on 24 April 1774 in Oraison in the Basses-Alpes. From 1782 he lived with his uncle, the canon of Riez, and studied first in Riez and later in Marseilles under the Oratorians. His father wished him to work in the Banque, but the experiment was unsuccessful and he returned to Riez for a further two years. During the French Revolution he found himself quite by chance at the military hospital in Soliers and, though he knew nothing about the subject at the start, soon developed a passionate interest in medicine. He studied under Larrey, the professor of anatomy, and at his suggestion competed successfully for the post of surgeon at the Val de Grâce. In 1796, French medicine was dominated by two men: Pinel who believed in the analytical approach of Condillac, and Corvisart who favoured observation based on clinical methods. Itard followed the former. After an accident one day in the Rue Saint-Jacques, the Director of the Institute there – the Abbé Sicard, Abbé de l'Epée's successor – called Itard to attend the patient, and some weeks later on 31 December 1800 invited him to become the chief physician at the Institution Imperiale des Sourds-Muets.

Itard, just twenty-five, was preparing a thesis on pneumothorax (submitted eventually in 1803) when the wild boy of Aveyron was discovered and brought to Paris on the orders of the Minister, Champagny, who realized the importance of the case for the study of man. The boy was entrusted to the Institute in the Rue Saint-Jacques, where Itard instantly decided to try and educate him. In 1801 he published a report on his strange pupil which made the child famous throughout Europe. The Czar of Russia sent Itard the gift of a valuable ring and, through his ambassador in Paris, offered him a lucrative post in St Petersburg, but Itard declined. Five years later, in 1806, at the invitation of the Ministry of the Interior, he produced a second report on the boy's progress, which was highly praised on behalf of the Institute by its permanent secretary Dacier. The report was written between June and September 1806 and published in 1807 'by government order' under Champagny's auspices.

Itard was a successful practitioner and lived in the centre of Paris where he saw private patients every morning, yet he returned each evening for consultations at the Deaf and Dumb Institute. He was an expert in many fields and wrote papers on hydropsy, hygiene, stammering, intermittent fevers, but particularly on speech training. In 1821 he became a member of the Académie de Médecine and published his famous *Traité des Maladies de l'Oreille et de l'Audition*, the most important study on this subject since the work written in 1683 by the otologist Duverney, who had been Bossuet's anatomy teacher. Itard reproved the scientists of his day for their neglect of the faculty of hearing, the understanding of which had not been noticeably advanced since the time of Galileo. He reviewed the existing works in the field, outlined a system of classification and suggested various new therapeutic techniques, notably catheterizing the Eustachian tube and perforating the tympanic membrane. He maintained, in opposition to the other specialists of the time, that deafness was not caused solely by paralysis of the auditory nerve, and also disproved the accepted view that deafness was always total. Using the results of careful experiments with the acoumeter, which he himself invented, Itard showed that most deaf patients display rudimentary hearing. He was, in short, the recognized founder of oto-rhyno-laryngology.

An educationalist's theoretical concern with physiology and medicine is very different from that of a practising specialist. Faced with the impossibility of curing deaf-mutes completely, Itard resolved, nevertheless, to teach them to speak as best he could. In the past, no thought had been given at all to the problem of educating these handicapped children. Together with Jacob Rodrigues Pereire, Itard applied his skills and his imagination to finding a solution. While most specialists advocated the use of sign-language and mime, he tried to cure dumbness orally with lip-reading, and in this was fifty years ahead of his time.

For almost forty years he devoted himself to the children at the Institute with an ability praised by all his colleagues. Although at the beginning of his career he had once bought a patent cure for deafness from a doctor in Bordeaux, he was always faithful to the principle that knowledge was advanced only with careful experiment. He believed that clarity could be achieved only through doubt and that intelligence was no use unless one recognized the limits of what one knew. He had no interest in financial success and gave up his town practice early in his career so that he could concentrate on his work in the Faubourg Saint-Jacques, where he saw his numerous patients in the morning, many of whose appointments had been made weeks in davance.

Itard continued to think about the boy from Aveyron long after his attempts to educate him were finished. Believing that dumbness was not purely organic in origin, he argued that a child would not learn to speak if its attentiveness was not sufficiently roused to listen to words, if its memory was not strong enough to retain them, or if the opportunity was lacking for constant repetition. Between 1822 and 1828 he published numerous papers, among them three for the Académie, and in 1831 published his book, *Mémoire sur le Mutisme Produit par la Lésion des Fonctions Intelléctuelles.*

He recognized the close relationship which exists between hearing and speaking, language and thought, culture and intelligence. He should be considered not only one of the first to attempt a cure for deaf-mutes but also as the founder of the education of backward children. In five years of experimentation with that special case, Victor, he invented many novel techniques for strengthening the boy's awareness of things and their relationships. In 1891 when Bourneville, the doctor for backward and neurotic children at the

Bicêtre asylum, decided to create a series of books on the education of abnormal children, he went on to publish the *Rapports et mémoires sur 'le Sauvage de l'Aveyron'*. Together with Esquirol, a friend and contemporary of the author, and Husson, Bousquet and Delasiauve, he maintained that 'Itard is justly recognized as a pioneer in the education of the mentally retarded.'

Itard was constantly quoted by Séguin, himself a specialist in the field of maladjusted children. Primarily a teacher, but also a doctor, Edouard Séguin spent ten years applying and modifying Itard's techniques at a school in the Rue Pigalle. He later emigrated to the USA, still faithful to his 'illustrious master', and founded a number of institutions for the mentally deficient, based on Itard's methods.[1]

In 1898, Maria Montessori,[2] the outstanding educationalist, discovered some forgotten works by Séguin, as well as those of Itard, and wrote of them:

The pedagogic writings of Itard are most interesting and minute descriptions of the educational efforts and experiences, and anyone reading them today must admit that they were practically the first attempts at experimental psychology. ... After this study of the methods in use in Europe I concluded my experiments upon the deficients in Rome. ... I followed Séguin's book and also derived much help from the remarkable experiments of Itard.

Guided by the work of these two men I had manufactured a great variety of didactic material. ... Having through actual experience justified my faith in Séguin's method I withdrew from active work among deficients and began a more thorough study of the works of Itard and Séguin. I felt the need of meditation. I did a thing I had not done before and which perhaps few students have been stirred to do – I translated into Italian and copied out with my own

1. In his *Traitement Moral, Hygiène, et Education des Idiots* (Paris 1846), Séguin discusses the work of his teacher. Other works on Itard's life and work include: Edouard Morel, 'Notice Biographique sur le Docteur Itard', *Annales de l'Education des Sourds-Muets* (Paris 1845), pp. 84–99; A. Bellanger, 'Le Docteur Itard', *Revue Générale de L'Enseignement des Sourds-Muets* (Paris, May 1904); A. Castex, 'Jean Itard, sa vie, son oeuvre', *Bulletin d'Oto-rhino-laryngologie*, September 1920; A. Porcher, 'Itard', *Revue Générale de L'Enseignement des Sourds-Muets*, June 1938, pp. 113–24, July–September 1938, pp. 129–32, and October 1938, pp. 1–6. Porcher includes a bibliography for Itard.

2. Maria Montessori, *The Montessori Method* (Frederick Stokes, New York 1912), pp. 34–41. She discusses the case of Victor, and Itard's educational theories.

hand the writings of these two men . . . making myself books as the old Bene-
dictine monks used to do before the diffusion of printing.

Alice Descoeudres, another advocate of the education of backward children, who had adapted the principles of Decroly, also
considered Itard's two reports 'a masterpiece'. She incorporated his
blindfold exercises and his techniques with the alphabet into her
own method of instruction and, following her master, invented
'mental orthopaedics' as an education for the senses. Though many
of his methods have now been superseded and though his whole
approach suffered perhaps from being too atomistic, Itard was
nonetheless responsible for the birth of an educational movement of
fundamental importance. He was without doubt one of the great
minds of the first half of the nineteenth century.

The modern world is a great exploiter of specialized labour.
Today when researchers have discovered the social causes of backwardness, when scientists and research institutions have switched
their attention from organic to psychological causes, Itard's importance is assured. The development of 'special education' and the
importance which the USA and the USSR attach to the problem
of mental deficiency – a crushing burden for any technological
civilization – give Itard's work a new meaning. People have come to
recognize the therapeutic possibilities of treatment. Charles, Clerk,
Guertin, McKay, Sarason and Spaulding have all shown that children dismissed as innate defectives can with patient instruction
achieve a degree of 'normality'. The Soviet psychologist Luria has
written: '. . . Hereditary forms of mental retardation are extremely
rare', an opinion propounded by Itard many years before. When
UNESCO published its *Statistical Report on Special Instruction* in
1961, its authors noted that 'the names which best evoke the general
character of the methods and techniques in use today are with some
exceptions those of the classical figures in education, many of whom
were pioneers of creative learning', and that 'there do not appear to
have been dramatic changes in this field since their time'. These
pioneers, among them Montessori and Descoeudres, of course made
modifications to Itard's theories but they preserved their content and

above all his basic principle that 'if a child knows the name or the natural sign of the objects he uses, if he knows the meaning of "yes" and "no" and can use them correctly, if he has the idea of doing better, then all is not lost'; in his *Discours to the Académie* Bousquet himself commended this belief which had been so rigorously observed by Victor's teacher.

Such was the outstanding career of the man, who, according to his contemporaries, resembled Henri IV in his appearance. His work was cut short by a premature illness and each summer after 1832 he accepted the advice of his friends and took long holidays at the resort of Beau-Séjour in Passy. A light-hearted youth was followed by a somewhat taciturn, though always kind and attentive, middle age. Itard had no illusions about his impending death and gave consideration to what would follow. In his will of October 1837 he left various possessions to his friends (he had never married); his library he gave to his nephew; an annual sum of a thousand francs was left to the Académie de Médecine for a 'prize to be awarded every three years for the best paper on applied medicine and therapeutic techniques'; and a much larger annual sum of eight thousand francs was given to the Institution des Sourds-Muets for the establishment of a 'complementary class', to be run on strictly oral principles so that the children whom he had helped in his lifetime with every scrap of his mental and physical strength would continue to be helped after his death. He died on 5 July 1838 at the age of sixty-four, as convinced as he had always been that 'nothing can protect man from the sad condition of his life which is suffering and death'. With his death, the world lost one of its greatest doctors, teachers and psychologists.

LUCIEN MALSON

Publisher's note: The text of Itard's Preface and his report, 'Of the First Developments of the Young Savage of Aveyron', are reprinted with slight alterations by kind permission of the Trustees of the British Museum. They are taken from an English translation published in 1802, entitled *An historical account of the discovery and education of A SAVAGE MAN, or of the first developments, physical and moral, of THE YOUNG SAVAGE caught in the woods near Aveyron, in the year 1798.*

Preface

Cast on this globe, without physical powers, and without innate ideas; unable by himself to obey the constitutional laws of his organization, which call him to the first rank in the system of being; MAN can find only in the bosom of society the eminent station that was destined for him in nature, and would be, without the aid of civilization, one of the most feeble and least intelligent of animals; – a truth which, although it has often been insisted upon, has not as yet been rigorously demonstrated. Those philosophers who have laid down the principles upon which it is founded; those who have afterwards supported and propagated it, have given, as a proof of it, the physical and moral state of some wandering tribes, whom they have regarded as not civilized at all, merely because they were not civilized in our particular manner: to these they had recourse, in order to become acquainted with the features of man in the pure state of nature. It is not, however, in these circumstances that we are to seek and study it. In the savage horde the most vagabond, as well as in the most civilized nations of Europe, man is only what he is made to be by his external circumstances; he is necessarily elevated by his equals; he contracts from them his habits and his wants; his ideas are no longer his own; he enjoys, from the enviable prerogative of his species, a capacity of developing his understanding by the power of imitation, and the influence of society.

We ought, then, to seek elsewhere the model of a man truly savage, of him who owes nothing to his equals; and to form our opinion of him from the particular histories of a small number of individuals, who, during the course of the seventeenth century, and at the beginning of the eighteenth, have been found, at different intervals, living in a state of solitude among the woods, where they had been abandoned at the most tender age.[1] But such was at these times the tardy progress of science, the students of which were devoted to theory and uncertain hypothesis, and to the exclusive labour of the closet, that actual observation was reckoned of no value; and these interesting facts tended little towards improving the natural history of man. Every thing that has been left of them by contemporary authors, is confined to some insignificant details, the most striking and general result of which is, that these individuals were not susceptible of any decidedly marked improvement; evidently for this reason, because to them was applied, without the slightest regard to the difference of their organs, the ordinary system of education. If this mode of instruction proved completely successful with the savage girl found in France towards the beginning of the last century, the reason is, that having lived in the woods with a companion, she was indebted already to this simple association for a certain development of her intellectual faculties. This was, in fact, an education such as Condillac[2] speaks of, when he supposes two children abandoned in a profound solitude, in whose case the sole influence of their cohabitation must give scope to the exercise of their memory and their imagination, and induce them to create a small number of artificial signs. It is an ingenious supposition; which is amply justified by the history of this same girl, whose memory was so far developed as to retrace various circumstances of her residence in the woods, and in the most minute manner, especially the violent death of her female companion.[3] Deprived of

1. Linnaeus makes the number amount to ten, and exhibits them as forming a variety of the human species (*Système de la Nature*).

2. Essai sur l'origine des connaissances humaines, part II, Section 1.

3. This girl was caught in the year 1731, in the environs of Châlons-sur-Marne, and educated in a convent, under the name of Mademoiselle Leblanc. She related as soon as she was able to speak, that she had lived in the woods with a companion, and that she had unfortunately killed her by a violent blow on the head one day, when, upon finding a chaplet under their feet, they disputed about the exclusive possession of it. – *Racine*, Poème de Religion.

This history, although it be very circumstantial, is nevertheless so ill told, that if one were to deduce from it, in the first place, what is insignificant, and, in the next, what is incredible, it presents only a very small number of particulars deserving notice; the most remarkable of which is the faculty which this young savage possessed, of recalling to her memory the circumstances of her previous condition.

these advantages, the rest of the children found in a state of individual insulation, brought into society faculties that were completely unsusceptible, which must baffle, supposing that they were directed towards their education, all the united efforts of a moral philosophy scarcely in its infancy, still entramelled with the prejudice of innate ideas, and by theories of medicine, the views of which, being necessarily contracted by a doctrine altogether mechanical, could not rise to philosophical reflections with regard to the maladies of the understanding. Assisted by the light of analysis, and lending to each other a mutual support, these two sciences have in our days got rid of their old errors, and made an immense progress towards perfection. On this account we have reason to hope, that, if ever a similar individual be presented to those of whom we have been speaking, they would *employ, in order to produce his physical and moral development, all the resources to be derived from their actual knowledge*: or, at least, if this application proved impossible or fruitless, there would be found in this age of observation some one individual, who, carefully *collecting the history of a being so astonishing, would ascertain what he is, and would infer, from what is wanting to him, the sum, as yet not calculated, of that knowledge and of those ideas for which man is indebted to his education.*

May I dare to confess that it is my intention to accomplish both of these important objects? But let me not be asked, if I have already been successful in the execution of my design? This would be a question very premature, to which I shall not be able to answer for a considerable time to come. Nevertheless I should have waited for it in silence, without wishing to occupy the public with an account of my labours, if it had not been as much my desire as it was my duty to prove, by the success of my first experiments, that the child on whom I have made them is not, as is generally believed, a hopeless idiot, but a being highly interesting, who deserves, in every point of view, the attention of observers, and the assiduities which are devoted to him by an enlightened and philanthropic administration.

Of the First Developments
of the
Young Savage of Aveyron

(*1799, printed 1801*)

A child, about eleven or twelve years of age, who had been seen some time before in the woods of Caune, in France, looking after acorns and roots, upon which he subsisted, was met in the same place, towards the close of the year 1798, by three sportsmen, who seized upon him at the instant he was climbing a tree to evade their pursuit. They conducted him to a neighbouring village, and put him under the care of an aged matron; from whom, however, before the end of a week, he contrived to escape, and fled to the mountains, where he wandered about during the severity of a most rigorous winter, clad only in a tattered shirt. At night he retired into solitary places, approaching, as the day advanced, the neighbouring villages; and in this manner he passed a vagrant kind of life, till the time in which, of his own accord, he sought refuge in a dwelling-house in the Canton of St Sernin. Here he was retained and taken care of for two or three days, and from thence was sent to the hospital of St Affrique, afterwards to Rodez, where he was kept for several months. During his abode in these different places, he appeared to be always equally wild, impatient of restraint, and capricious in his temper, continually endeavouring to get away, affording materials for the most interesting observations, which were collected by a person worthy of the utmost credit, and which I shall not fail to relate in those parts of the following Essay where they may be most advantageously introduced.[1] A clergyman, distinguished as a patron of science and general literature, conceiving that, from this event, some new light might be thrown on the moral science of man, obtained permission for the child to be brought to Paris. He arrived there about the end of the year 1799, under the care of a poor but respectable old man, who, being obliged to leave him soon after, promised to return, and be a father to him, if, at any time, he should be abandoned by society.

The most brilliant but unreasonable expectations were formed by the people of Paris respecting the Savage of Aveyron, before he arrived.[2] Many curious people anticipated great pleasure in beholding what would be his astonishment at the sight of all the fine things in the capital. On the other hand, many persons eminent for their superior understanding, forgetting that our organs are less flexible, and imitation more difficult, in proportion as man is removed from society, and the period of his infancy, thought that the education of this individual would be the business of only a few months, and that they should very soon hear him make the most striking observations concerning his past manner of life. Instead of this, what did they see? – a disgusting, slovenly boy, affected with spasmodic, and frequently with convulsive motions, continually balancing himself like some of the animals in the menagerie, biting and scratching those who contradicted him, expressing no kind of affection for those who attended upon him; and, in short, indifferent to every body, and paying no regard to any thing.

It may be easily imagined that a being of this nature would excite only a momentary curiosity. People came together in crowds; they saw him, without properly observing him; they passed their judg-

1. All that I shall hereafter say respecting the history of this child before his abode in the capital, is authenticated by the official communications of Citizens Guirauld and Constant of St Festêve, commissaries of government; the former in the Canton of St Affrique, the latter in that of St Sernier; and from the observations of Citizen Bonnaterre, Professor of Natural History in the central school of the Department of Aveyron.

2. If, by the expression *savage*, we generally understand a man but a little civilized it will be allowed that he, who is so in no degree whatever, still more rigorously deserves that denomination. I shall continue therefore to apply this name to him until I have explained the motives which have determined me to give him another.

ment on him, without knowing him; and spoke no more on the subject. In the midst of this general indifference, the administrators of the National Institute for the Deaf and Dumb, and its celebrated director, did not forget, that society, in drawing to herself this unfortunate youth, had contracted towards him indispensable obligations which she was bound to fulfil. Entering, then, into the hopes which I had conceived from a course of medical treatment, they determined that he should be entrusted to my care.

Before I present to the reader the particulars and results of this measure, I must state the point from which we set out, recall and describe the first stages, in order the better to appreciate the value of the progress we have already made; and, by thus opposing the past to the present, we may be better able to ascertain what may be expected in future. Obliged, then, to return to facts already known, I shall unfold them in few words; and, that I may not labour under the suspicion of having exaggerated them with a view of enhancing the importance of those which I shall oppose to them, I may be excused if I give an analytical description of the case, which a physician, as highly esteemed for his genius and skill in observation, as for his profound knowledge in the diseases of the mind, read to a learned society, to which I had the honour of being admitted.

Beginning with an account of the sensorial functions of the young savage, Citizen Pinel represented to us his senses as in such a state of inertia, that this unfortunate youth was found, according to his report, very inferior to some of our domestic animals. His eyes were without steadiness, without expression, wandering from one object to another, without fixing upon any thing; so little instructed in other respects, and so little experienced in the sense of touch, that he was unable to distinguish between an object in relief and a paint-ing: the organ of hearing was alike insensible to the loudest noises and to the most charming music: that of the voice was still more imperfect, uttering only a guttural and uniform sound: his sense of smell was so little cultivated, that he seemed to be equally indifferent to the odour of the finest perfumes, and to the most fetid exhala-tions; finally, the sense of feeling was limited to those mechanical functions which arose from the dread of objects which might be in his way.

Proceeding to the state of the intellectual faculties of this child, the author of the report exhibited him to us as incapable of attention (unless as it respected the objects of his wants) and consequently of all the operations of the mind which depended upon it; destitute of memory, of judgment, even of a disposition to imitation; and so bounded were his ideas, even those which related to his immediate wants, that he could not open a door, nor get on a chair to obtain the food which was put out of the reach of his hand; in short, destitute of every means of communication, attaching neither expression nor intention to the gestures and motions of his body, passing with rapidity, and without any apparent motive, from a state of profound melancholy, to bursts of the most immoderate laughter; insensible to every species of moral affection, his discernment was never excited but by the stimulus of gluttony; his pleasure, an agreeable sensation of the organs of taste, his intelligence, a susceptibility of producing incoherent ideas, connected with his physical wants; in a word, his whole existence was a life purely animal.

Afterwards, reciting many histories collected at Bicêtre, of children incurably affected with idiotism, Citizen Pinel established the most striking resemblance between the situation of these unfortunate persons, and that of the child which occupied our present attention; from which he drew, as a necessary consequence, that a perfect identity existed between these young idiots, and the Savage of Aveyron. This identity led to the inevitable conclusion, that a person labouring under an affliction, hitherto considered as incurable, was unsusceptible of every species of sociability and instruction. Such was also the consequence deduced by Citizen Pinel, and which he nevertheless accompanied with that philosophical doubt, conspicuous in all his writings, and which shews, in his presages, that he knows how to appreciate the science of prognosis, and that he regarded this case as affording only uncertain probabilities and conjectures.

I did not assent to this unfavourable opinion; and, in spite of the truth of the picture, and the justness of the representations, I conceived some hopes, which were grounded on the two-fold consideration of the *cause*, and the *possibility of curing* this apparent idiotism. I could not proceed without stopping an instant to dwell upon these two considerations. They still bear on the present moment; they result from a series of facts which I am going to relate, and in which I shall be obliged to mix frequently my own reflections.

If it was proposed to resolve the following metaphysical problem, viz. '*to determine what would be the degree of understanding, and the nature of the ideas of a youth, who, deprived, from his infancy, of all education, should have lived entirely separated from individuals of his species*'; I am strangely deceived, or the solution of the problem would give to this individual an understanding connected only with a small number of his wants, and deprived, by his insulated condition, of all those simple and complex ideas which we receive from education, and which are combined in our minds in so many different ways, by means only of our knowledge of signs. Well! the moral picture of this youth would be that of the Savage of Aveyron, and the solution of the problem would give the measure and cause of his intellectual state.

But to admit, with still more reason, the existence of this cause, we must prove that it has operated a number of years: And to reply to the objection which may be made, and which indeed has been already started, that the pretended Savage was only a poor silly child, whom his parents, in disgust, had lately abandoned altogether at the entrance of the woods – if those who maintained this opinion had observed him within a short time after his arrival at Paris, they would have seen that all his habits bore the stamp of a wandering and solitary life; an unconquerable aversion from society and its customs, from our clothes, our furniture, our apartments, and modes of preparing our food; a complete indifference towards the objects of our pleasures, and our factitious wants; – an empassioned taste for the liberty of the fields; so much alive to his past situation, in spite of his new wants, and his growing affections, that during a short stay which he made at Montmorenci, he would have infallibly escaped into the forest but for the most severe precautions; and twice he did get from the hospital of the deaf and dumb, notwithstanding the watchfulness of his attendant; – an extraordinary swiftness; slow, indeed, as long as he wore shoes and stockings, but always remarkable for the difficulty with which he conformed to our grave and measured mode of walking, and for the perpetual propensity that he shewed to set off on a trot or gallop; – an obstinate habit of smelling at every thing which came in his way, even bodies which to us appeared inodorous; – a mastication, not less astonishing, uniformly executed by the hasty action of the cutting teeth, sufficiently indicating, by its analogy with some other animals, that our savage lived chiefly on vegetable productions; I say chiefly, because it appears, by the following trait, that, under certain circumstances, he would have made a prey of small animals deprived of life: A dead canary-bird was one day given him, and in an instant he stripped off its feathers, great and small, tore it open with his nails, smelt it, and threw it away.

Other indications of an isolated, precarious and wandering life, were deduced from the nature and number of the scars with which the body of this child was covered. Without mentioning that which was seen on the fore-part of his neck, and of which I shall take notice hereafter, as coming from another cause, and deserving particular attention, we reckoned four on the face, six along the left arm, three at some distance from the left shoulder, four at the circumference of the pubis, one on his left thigh, three on one leg, and two on the other; which together make twenty-three scars. – Some of these appeared to have come from the bites of animals, others from scratches and excoriations, more or less large and deep; numerous and indelible testimonies of a long and total abandonment of this unfortunate youth, and which, considered under a point of view more general and philosophical, bear witness as much against the weakness and insufficiency of man, given over wholly to his own resources, as they are favourable to the resources of Nature, which, according to laws apparently contradictory, labours openly to renew and preserve that which she tends secretly to waste and destroy. If we add to all these facts, taken from observation, those, not less authentic, which the country people witnessed, who lived in the vicinity of the woods in which the child was discovered, we shall find that, when he was first taken into society, he lived on acorns, potatoes, and raw chestnuts; that he was unable to utter any sort of sound; that in spite of the most active vigilance he was many times very near escaping; that he exhibited, at first, great unwillingness to lie in a bed, etc. We shall find, moreover, that he had been seen more than five years before, entirely naked, and flying at the approach of men; which supposes that he had been already, at his first appearance, habituated to that kind of life, which could not be the result only of an abode of two years or less, in uninhabited places. Thus this child passed, in an absolute solitude, almost seven years out of twelve, which appeared to be his age when he was caught in the woods of Caune. It is therefore probable, and almost certain, that he had been abandoned when he was about four or five years old; and if, at that period, he had already obtained some ideas, and the knowledge of some words, as the beginning of education, these would have been obliterated from his memory in consequence of his insulated situation.

This then appears to me to be the cause of his present state, from which it will be seen that I entertain considerable hopes for the success of my cares. Indeed, when we consider the little time he has been in society, the Savage of Aveyron is much less like a simple youth, than an infant of ten or twelve months old, and an infant who should have against him anti-social habits, an obstinate inattention, organs scarcely flexible, and a very blunted sensibility. In this last point of view his situation became a case purely medical; and the treatment of it belonged to moral medicine – to that sublime art created by the Willis's and the Crichtons of England, and lately introduced into France by the success and writings of Professor Pinel.

Guided by the spirit of their doctrine much less than by their precepts, which could not be adapted to this unforeseen case, I reduced to five principal heads the moral treatment or education of the Savage of Aveyron. My objects were,

1. To attach him to social life, by rendering it more pleasant to him than that which he was then leading, and, above all, more analogous to the mode of existence that he was about to quit.

2. To awaken the nervous sensibility by the most energetic stimulants, and sometimes by lively affections of the mind.

3. To extend the sphere of his ideas, by giving him new wants, and by increasing the number of his relations to the objects surrounding him.

4. To lead him to the use of speech by subjecting him to the necessity of imitation.

5. To exercise frequently the most simple operations of the mind upon the objects of his physical wants; and, at length, by inducing the application of them to objects of instruction.

SECTION I. My first object was *to attach him to social life, by rendering it more pleasant to him than that which he was then leading, and, above all, more analogous to the mode of existence that he was about to quit.*

The suddenness of the change in his manner of life, the frequent importunities of the curious, some bad treatment, the inevitable effects of his living with children of his own age, seemed to have extinguished all hopes of his civilization. His petulant activity of mind had insensibly degenerated into a dull apathy, which produced habits still more solitary. Thus, excepting those moments in which hunger led him to the kitchen, he was almost always to be found squatting in a corner of the garden, or concealed in the second storey of some ruinous buildings. In this deplorable situation he was seen by some people from Paris, who, after a very short examination, adjudged him to be only fit to be sent to Bedlam; as if society had a right to take a child from a free and innocent life, and dismiss him to die of melancholy in a mad-house, that he might thus expiate the misfortune of having disappointed public curiosity. I thought that a more simple, and, what is of still greater importance, a much more humane course should be taken, which was to treat him kindly, and to yield a ready compliance with his taste and inclinations. Madame Guérin, to whose particular care the administration had entrusted this child, acquitted herself, and still discharges this arduous task, with all the patience of a mother, and the intelligence of an enlightened instructor. So far from directly opposing his habits, she knew how, in some measure, to comply with them; and thus to answer the object proposed in our first general head.

If one may judge of the past life of this child, by his present dispositions, we may conclude that, like some savages in the warmer climates, he was acquainted with four circumstances only; to sleep, to eat, to do nothing, and to run about in the fields. To make him happy, then, after his own manner, it was necessary to put him to bed at the close of the day, to furnish him abundantly with food adapted to his taste, to bear with his indolence, and to accompany him in his walks, or rather in his races in the open air, and this whenever he pleased. These rural excursions appeared to him even more agreeable when any sudden and violent change in the atmosphere took place; so true it is, that, in every condition, man is delighted with new sensations. As, for example, when he has been observed, within his chamber, he was seen rocking backwards and forwards with a tiresome uniformity, directing his eyes constantly towards the window, and casting them in a melancholy manner on the external air. If, at any time, a boisterous wind arose; if the sun, concealed behind a cloud, suddenly burst forth, brilliantly illuminating the surrounding atmosphere, he expressed an almost convulsive joy by thundering peals of laughter; during which, all his turnings, backwards and forwards, resembled very much a kind of leap which he wished to take, to throw himself out of the window into the garden. Sometimes, instead of joyful emotions, he exhibited a species of madness; he wrung his hands, applied his fists to his eyes, gnashed his teeth, and became formidable to persons about him. One morning, after a heavy fall of snow, as soon as he awaked, he uttered a cry of joy, leaped from his bed, ran to the window, afterwards to the door, going backwards and forwards, from one to the other, with the greatest impatience, and, at length, escaped half-dressed into the garden. There he exhibited the utmost emotions of pleasure; he ran, rolled himself in the snow, and taking it up by handfuls, devoured it with an incredible avidity.

But he did not always manifest such lively and boisterous expressions of joy at the sight of the grand phenomena of Nature. In some cases they appeared to induce the quiet expression of sorrow and melancholy; a remark hazarded in opposition to the opinions of metaphysicians, but which we could not avoid making, when we observed this unfortunate youth, with attention, under the operation of certain circumstances. When the severity of the season drove every other person out of the garden, he delighted in taking a great many turns about it; after which he used to seat himself on the edge of a bowl of water. I have often stopped for whole hours together, and, with unspeakable pleasure, to examine him in this situation; to observe how all his convulsive motions, and that continual rocking of his whole body diminished, and by degrees subsided, to give place to a more tranquil attitude; and how insensibly his face, insignificant or distorted as it might be, took the well-defined character of sorrow, or melancholy reverie, in proportion as his eyes were steadily fixed on the surface of the water, and when he threw into it, from time to time, some remains of withered leaves. When, in a moon-light night, the rays of that luminary penetrated into his room, he seldom failed to awake out of his sleep, and to place himself before the window. There he remained, during a part of the night, standing motionless, his neck extended, his eyes fixed towards the country illuminated by the moon, and, carried away in a sort of contemplative extasy, the silence of which was interrupted only by deep-drawn inspirations, after considerable intervals, and which were always accompanied with a feeble and plaintive sound.

It would have been as useless, as inhuman, to oppose these habits; and I wished to associate them with his new existence, in order to render it more agreeable to him. This was not the case with those which laboured under the disadvantage of continually exercising his stomach and muscles, and of course leaving, in a state of in-action, the sensibility of the nerves, and the faculty of the brain. Thus, I endeavoured, and was gradually successful, in my attempts to render his excursions less frequent, his meals less copious, and repeated after longer intervals, the time he spent in bed much shorter, and his exercise more subservient to his instruction.

SECTION II. My second object was *to awaken the nervous sensibility by the most powerful stimulants, and sometimes by lively affections of the mind.*

Some modern physiologists have presumed, that sensibility is in exact proportion to the degree of civilization. I do not think that a stronger proof can be given in favour of this opinion, than the small degree of sensibility in the sensorial organs, which was observable in the case of the Savage of Aveyron. We may be perfectly satisfied, merely by casting our eyes over the description that I have already exhibited, and which is founded on facts that I have derived from the most authentic sources. I shall here add, in connection with the same subject, some of my own most interesting and important observations.

Frequently, during the course of the winter, I have seen him, whilst he was amusing himself in the garden belonging to the asylum of the Deaf and Dumb, suddenly squat down, half naked, on the wet turf, and remain exposed in this way, for hours together, to wind and rain. It was not only to the cold, but also to the most violent heat, that his skin, and sense of touch, shewed no kind of sensibility. It frequently happened, when he was near the fire, and live coals have fallen out of the grate, that he snatched them up, and threw them back again with the most perfect indifference. We have more than once found him in the kitchen, taking away, in the same manner, potatoes out of the boiling water, and I know that he had, at that time, a skin of very fine and delicate texture.[3] I have often given

3. I gave him, said a person, who had seen him at St Sernin, a great quantity of potatoes; he seemed to be pleased at the sight, laid hold of them with his hands, and threw them into the fire. He took them back again soon after, and ate them quite burning hot.

him large quantities of snuff, without exciting any disposition to sneeze; which is a perfect proof, that in this case there did not exist between the organ of smell, and those of respiration and sight, that kind of sympathy which is apt to induce either sneezing, or the secretion of tears. This last symptom was still less liable than the other to be produced by painful affections of the mind; and in spite of numberless contradictions; in spite of the severe and apparently cruel measures made use of, especially during the first months of his new life, I never once caught him in the act of shedding tears.

Of all his senses, his ear seemed to be the most completely insensible. But it was remarkable that the noise occasioned by the cracking of a walnut, a fruit of which he was particularly fond, never failed to awaken his attention. The truth of this observation may be depended upon: and yet this very organ betrayed an insensibility to the loudest noises, to the explosions, for instance, of fire-arms. I one day fired two pistols close by his ear; the first produced some emotion, but the second merely made him turn his head with apparent indifference.

Thus in selecting some such cases as this, in which the defect of attention, on the part of the mind, might appear like a want of sensibility in the particular organ, it was found, contrary to first appearances, that this nervous power was remarkably feeble in almost all the senses. Of course it made part of my plan to develop the sensibility by every possible means, and to lead the mind to a habit of attention, by exposing the senses to the reception of the most lively impressions.

Of the different means which I made use of, the effect of heat appeared to me to accomplish in the most effectual manner the object I had in view. It is an idea admitted by physiologists,[4] and men learned in political science, that the inhabitants of the southern climates are indebted to the action of heat, on the surface of the skin, for that exquisite sensibility which is superior to theirs who

4. *Lacuse*, Idée de l'homme physique et moral; *Laroche*, Analyse des fonctions du système énerveux; *Fouquet*, article on 'Sensibilité' in the *Encyclopédie*; *Montesquieu*, Esprit des Lois, Book XIV.

live in the northern regions. I made use of this stimulus in every kind of way. I did not think it sufficient to provide him with comfortable clothing, a warm bed and lodging room, but I thought it likewise necessary to put him in the hot bath for two or three hours every day, during which, water at the same temperature as that of the bath was frequently dashed on his head. I did not observe that the heat and repetition of the bathings were followed by their usual debilitating effect which might have been expected. I wished that this might have happened, being perfectly convinced that, in such a case, the loss of muscular force is advantageous to the nervous sensibility. At any rate, if this subsequent effect did not take place, the first did not disappoint my expectation. After some time our young savage appeared evidently sensible to the action of cold – made use of his hand in order to ascertain the temperature of the bath, and would not go into it if it was not sufficiently warm. The same cause led him very soon to appreciate the utility of that clothing to which before he barely submitted. As soon as he appeared to perceive the advantage of clothes, there was but a single step necessary to oblige him to dress himself. This end was obtained, in a few days, by leaving him every morning exposed to the cold within the reach of his clothes, until he found out the method of putting them on himself. An expedient very similar effected the purpose of leading him into habits of neatness and cleanliness; as the certainty of passing the night in a cold and wet bed induced the necessity of his rising in order to satisfy his natural wants.

In addition to the use of the warm bath, I prescribed the application of dry frictions to the spinal vertebrae, and even the tickling of the lumbar regions. This last mean seemed to have the most stimulating tendency: I found myself under the necessity of forbidding the use of it, when its effects were no longer confined to the production of pleasurable emotions; but appeared to extend themselves to the organs of generation, and to indicate some danger of awakening the sensations of premature puberty.

To these various stimulants I thought it right to call in aid the excitement produced by the mental affections. Those of which alone he was susceptible, at this period, were confined to two: joy and anger. I provoked the latter, only at distant intervals, in order that the paroxysm might, by that means, be more violent, and always be attended with a plausible semblance of justice. I sometimes remarked, that, at the moment of his most violent indignation, his understanding seemed to acquire a temporary enlargement, which suggested to him some ingenious expedient for freeing himself from disagreeable embarrassment. Once as we were endeavouring to persuade him to make use of the bath, when it was only moderately warm, our repeated and urgent entreaties threw him into a violent passion. In this temper, perceiving that his gouvernante was not at all convinced, by the frequent trials which he had himself made with his fingers, of the coldness of the water, he turned back towards her in a precipitate manner, seized her hand, and plunged it with his own into the bath.

To mention another instance of this nature: one day as he was in my study, seated on an ottoman, I placed myself by his side, and between us a Leyden phial, slightly charged; a trifling shock that he received from it diverted him from his state of reverie. On observing the uneasiness which he expressed at the approach of this instrument, I thought that he would be induced, in order to remove it to a greater distance, to lay hold of the knob; he adopted a measure much more prudent, which was, to thrust his hands into the opening of his waistcoat, and retire a few inches, till his thigh was no longer in contact with the outer coating of the bottle. I drew near him a second time, and again placed the phial between us; this occasioned another movement on his part, and that another on mine. This little stratagem lasted till driven to the farther end of the sofa, and restricted by the wall behind, before by a table, and on my side by the troublesome machine, it was no longer possible for him to perform another movement. He then seizing the moment when I was advancing my arm to lay hold of his, very dextrously put my wrist on the knob of the jar; I of course, instead of him, received the discharge.

But if, at any time, in spite of the lively interest and affection which I felt for this young orphan, I thought it right to awaken his anger, I permitted not a single opportunity to escape me of affording him enjoyment; and it must be confessed that, in order to succeed in this, there was no necessity of having recourse to any means that were attended with difficulty or expense. A ray of the sun, received on a mirror, reflected in his chamber, and thrown on the ceiling; a glass of water, which was made to fall, drop by drop, from a certain height, on the end of his fingers whilst he was bathing; and even a little milk, contained in a wooden porringer, which was placed at the farther end of his bath, and which the oscillations of the water moved about, excited in him lively emotions of joy, which were expressed by shouts and the clapping of his hands: these were very nearly all the means necessary in order to enliven and delight, often almost to intoxication, this simple child of nature.

Such were, among a multitude of others, the stimulants, as well physical as moral, with which I laboured to develop the sensibility of his organs. These means produced, after the short space of three months, a general excitement of all his sensitive powers. By that time the touch shewed itself sensible to the impression of all bodies, whether warm or cold, smooth or rough, soft or hard. At that period I wore a pair of velvet pantaloons, over which he seemed to take a pleasure in drawing his hand. It was by his touch that he generally ascertained whether his potatoes were sufficiently boiled: he took them from the bottom of the pot with a spoon; he then laid hold of them, repeatedly, with his fingers, and afterwards decided, from the degree of hardness or softness, whether to eat them or to throw them back into the boiling water. When a piece of paper was given him to light a candle, he seldom waited till the wick caught fire, but hastily threw away the paper before the flame was near touching his fingers. After having been induced to push or to carry a body that was either hard or heavy, he seldom failed to draw away his hands on a sudden, to look attentively at the end of his fingers, although they were not in the slightest degree bruised or wounded, and to put them in a leisurely manner in the opening of his waistcoat. The sense of smell had been, in a similar manner, improved in consequence of the change which had taken place in his constitution. The least irritation applied to this organ excited sneezing; and, I presumed, from the horror with which he was seized the first time that this happened, that it was a thing altogether new to him. He was so much agitated as even to throw himself on his bed.

The improvement of the sense of taste was still more remarkable. The articles of food with which this child was fed, for a little time after his arrival at Paris, were shockingly disgusting. He trailed them about the room, and eat them out of his hands that were besmeared with filth. But at the period of which I am now speaking, he constantly threw away, in a pot, the contents of his plate, if any particle of dirt or dust had fallen upon it; and, after he had broken his walnuts under his feet, he took pains to clean them in the nicest and most delicate manner.

At length diseases, even the diseases which are the inevitable and troublesome results arising from a state of civilization, added their testimony to the development of the principle of life. Very early in the spring our young savage was affected with a violent cold, and some weeks after, with two attacks of a similar nature, one almost immediately succeeding the other.

These symptoms, however, were confined only to some of the organs; those of the sight and hearing were not at all affected by them: evidently because these two senses, being much less simple than the rest, required a minute and more protracted education, as will appear from the sequel of this history. The simultaneous improvement of three senses, that was produced in consequence of the stimulants applied to the skin, at the same time that these two last remained stationary, is an important fact, and deserves a particular attention from physiologists. It seems to prove, what from other sources appeared not improbable, that the sense of touch, of smell, and of taste, are merely different modifications of the organ of the skin; whilst those of the ear and the eye, being less exposed to external impressions, and enveloped with a covering much more complicated, are subject to other laws of amelioration, and ought, on that account, to be considered as constituting a class perfectly distinct.

SECTION III. My third object was *to extend the sphere of his ideas, by giving him new wants, and multiplying his relations and connections with surrounding objects.*

If the progress of this child towards civilization; if my success in developing his intelligence has been hitherto so slow and difficult, it ought to be attributed to the almost innumerable obstacles which I have had to encounter in accomplishing this third object. I have given him successively toys of every sort; more than once, for whole hours, I have endeavoured to make him acquainted with the use of them, and I have had the mortification to observe, that, so far from interesting his attention, these various objects only tended to excite fretfulness and impatience; so much so, that he was continually endeavouring to conceal or destroy them when a favourable opportunity occurred. As an instance of this disposition, after having been some time confined in his chair, with nine-pins placed before him, in order to amuse him in that situation; in consequence of being irritated by this kind of restraint that was imposed upon him, he took it into his head, one day, as he was alone in the chamber, to throw them into the fire; before the flames of which he was immediately after found warming himself, with an expression of great delight.

However, I invented some means of attaching him to certain amusements, which were connected with his appetite for food. One, for instance, I often procured him, at the end of a meal, when I took him to dine with me in the city. I placed before him, without any regular order, and in an inverted position, several little silver goblets, under one of which I put a chestnut. Being convinced of having attracted his attention, I raised them, one after another, with the exception of that only which enclosed the chestnut. After having thus proved to him that they contained nothing, and having replaced them in the same order, I invited him, by signs, to seek in his turn for the chestnut; the first goblet on which he cast his eyes was precisely that under which I had concealed the little recompense of his attention. This was only a very simple effort of memory: but by degrees I rendered the amusement more complicated. After having, by the same process, concealed another chestnut, I changed the order of all the goblets, in a manner, however, rather slow, in order that, in this general inversion, it might be less difficult for him to follow with his eyes, and with attention, that particular one which concealed the precious deposit. I did more; I put something under three of these goblets, and yet his attention, although divided between three objects, did not fail to pursue them in all the changes of the situation. This is not all; – this was not the only object I intended to obtain. The discernment which he exhibited, in this instance, was excited merely by the instinct of gluttony. In order to render his attention less interested, and in a certain degree less animal, I deducted from this amusement every thing which had any connection with his palate, and I afterwards put nothing under the goblets that was eatable. The result of this experiment was very nearly as satisfactory as of the former; and this stratagem afforded nothing more than a simple amusement: it was not, however, without being of considerable use, in exciting the exercise of his judgment, and inducing a habit of fixed attention.

With the exception of these sorts of diversion, which, like those that have been already mentioned, were intimately connected with his physical wants, it has been impossible for me to inspire him with a taste for those which are natural to his age. I am absolutely certain, that, if I could have effected this, I should have derived from it unspeakable assistance. In order to be convinced of the justness of this idea, we need only attend to the powerful influence which is produced upon the first developments of the mind, by the plays of infancy, as well as the various little pleasures of the palate.

I did every thing in order to awaken these last inclinations, by offering him those dainties which are most coveted by children, and from which I hoped to derive important advantage; as they afforded me new means of reward, of punishment, of encouragement, and of instruction. But the aversion he expressed for all sweetmeats, and the most tender and delicate viands, was insurmountable. I then thought it right to try the use of highly stimulating food, as better adapted to excite a sense which was necessarily blunted by the habit of feeding upon grosser aliments. I did not succeed better in this trial; I offered to him, in vain, even during those moments when he felt the most extreme hunger and thirst, strong liquors, and dishes richly seasoned with all kinds of spices. At length, despairing of being able to inspire him with any new taste, I made the most of the small number of those to which his appetite was confined, by endeavouring to accompany them with all the necessary circumstances which might increase the pleasure that he derived from indulging himself in them. It was with this view that I often took him to dine with me in the city. On these days there was placed on the table a complete collection of his most favourite dishes. The first time that he was at such a feast, he expressed transports of joy, which rose almost to frenzy: no doubt he thought he should not sup so well as he had dined; for he did not scruple to carry away, in the evening, on his leaving the house, a plate of lentils which he had stolen from the kitchen: I felt great satisfaction at the result of this first excursion. I had found out a *pleasure* for him; I had only to repeat it a certain number of times in order to convert it into a *want*; this is what I actually effected. I did more; I took care that these excursions should always be preceded by certain preliminaries which might be remarked by him: this I did, by going into his room about four o'clock, with my hat on my head, and his shirt held in my hand. Very soon these preparations were considered as the signal of departure. At the moment I appeared, I was understood; he dressed himself in great haste, and followed me, with expressions of uncommon satisfaction and delight. I do not give this fact as a proof of a superior intelligence, since there is nobody that might not object that the most common dog is capable of doing as much. But even admitting this mental equality between the boy and the brute, we must at least allow that an important change had taken place; and those who had seen the Savage of Aveyron, immediately after his arrival at Paris, know that he was vastly inferior, with regard to discernment, to the more intelligent of our domestic animals.

I found it impossible, when I took him out with me, to keep him in proper order in the streets: it was necessary for me either to go on the full trot with him, or make use of the most violent force, in order to compel him to walk at the same moderate pace with myself. Of course we were, in future, obliged to go out in a carriage: this was another new pleasure which attached him more and more to his frequent excursions. In a short time these days ceased to be merely days of feasting, in which he gave himself up to the most lively joy; they absolutely became real wants: the deprivation of which, when the interval between them was made a little longer than usual, rendered him low spirited, restless and fretful.

What an increase of pleasure was it to him when our visits were paid to the country! I took him not long ago to the seat of Citizen Lachabeaussière, in the vale of Montmorence. It was a very curious and exceedingly interesting spectacle, to observe the joy which was painted in his eyes, in all the motions and postures of his body, at the view of the hills and the woods of this charming valley: it seemed as if the doors of the carriages were a restraint upon the eagerness of his feelings; he inclined sometimes towards the one and sometimes towards the other, and betrayed the utmost impatience, when the horses happened to go slower than usual, or stopped for a short time. He spent two days at this rural mansion; such was here the influence upon his mind, arising from the exterior agency of these woods, and these hills, with which he could not satiate his sight, that he appeared more than ever restless and savage; and in spite of the most assiduous attention that was paid to his wishes, and the most affectionate regard that was expressed for him, he seemed to be occupied only with an anxious desire of taking his flight. Altogether engrossed by this prevailing idea, which in fact absorbed all the faculties of his mind, and the consciousness even of his physical wants, and, rising from table every minute, he ran to the window, with a view, if it was open, of escaping into the park; or, if it were not, to contemplate, at least, through it, all those objects towards which he was irresistibly attracted, by recent habits, and, perhaps, also by the remembrance of a life independent, happy, and regretted. On this account, I determined no longer to subject him to similar trials; but, that he might not be entirely secluded from an opportunity of gratifying his rural taste, I still continued to take him out to walk in some gardens in the neighbour-hood, the formal and regular dispositions of which have nothing in common with those sublime landscapes that are exhibited in wild and uncultivated nature, and which so strongly attach the savage to the scenes of his infancy. On this account Madam Guérin some-times took him to the Luxembourg, and almost every day to the garden belonging to the observatory, where the obliging civility of Citizen Lemeri allowed him to take a daily repast of milk.

In consequence of these new habits, some recreations of his own choice, and all the tender attentions that were shewn him, in his present situation, he at length began to acquire a fondness for it. Hence arose that lively attachment which he feels for his gouvernante, and which he sometimes expresses to her in the most affecting manner. He never leaves her without evident uneasiness, not ever meets her without expressions of satisfaction. Once, after having slipped from her in the streets, on seeing her again he burst into a flood of tears. For some hours he still continued to shew a deep drawn and interrupted respiration, and a pulse in a kind of febrile state. Madam Guérin having then addressed him in rather a reproachful manner, he was again overwhelmed with tears. The friendship which he feels for me is much weaker, as might naturally have been expected. The attentions which Madam Guérin pays him are of such a nature, that their value may be appreciated at the moment; those cares, on the contrary, which I devote to him, are of distant and insensible utility. It is evident that this difference arises from the cause which I point out, as I am myself indulged with hours of favourable reception; they are those which I have never dedicated to his improvement. For instance, if I go to his chamber, in the evening, when he is about to retire to rest, the first thing that he does is to prepare himself for my embrace; then draw me to him, by laying hold of my arm, and making me sit on his bed. Then in general he seizes my hand, draws it over his eyes, his forehead, and the back part of his head, and detains it with his own, a long time, applied to those parts.

People may say what they please, but I will ingenuously confess, that I submit, without reluctance, to all these little marks of infantine fondness. Perhaps I shall be understood by those who consider how much effect is produced upon the mind of an infant, by compliances, apparently trivial, and small marks of that tenderness which nature hath implanted in the heart of a mother; the expression of which excites the first smiles, and awakens the earliest joys of life.

SECTION IV. My fourth object was, *to lead him to the use of speech, by subjecting him to the necessity of imitation.*

If I had wished to have published only successful experiments, I should have suppressed this fourth section from my work, as well the means which I made use of in order to accomplish my object, as well as the little advantage which I derived from them. But my intention is not to give the history of my own labours, but merely that of the progressive developments which appeared in the mind of the Savage of Aveyron; and, of course, I ought not to omit any thing that can throw light on his moral history. I shall be even obliged to advance, on this occasion, some theoretical ideas; and I hope I shall be pardoned for doing so, when it is considered what attention I have paid, that they should be supported upon facts, as well as the necessity under which I felt myself of answering such enquiries as these: '*Does the savage speak?*' '*If he is not deaf, why does he not speak?*'

It may easily be conceived, that, in the bosom of forests, and far from the society of every rational being, the ear of our savage was not in the way of experiencing any other impression than those which were made upon it by a very small number of sounds, which were in general connected with his physical wants. It was not, in such a situation, an organ which discriminates the various articulate modifications of the human voice: it was there simply an instrument of self preservation, which informed him of the approach of a dangerous animal, or of the fall of some wild fruit. It is evident, that the ear is confined to certain offices, when we consider the little or no impression which was produced upon this organ, for a whole year, by all the sounds and noises which did not interest his own particular wants; and, on the other hand, the exquisite irritability which this sense exhibited with regard to those things that had any relation to his necessities. When, without his knowing of it, I plucked, in the most cautious and gentle manner, a chestnut or walnut: – when I only touched the key of the door which held him captive, he never failed instantly to turn back, and run towards the place whence the noise arose. If the hearing did not express the same susceptibility for the sounds of the human voice, for the explosion even of fire-arms, it may be accounted for from that organ being little sensible and attentive to any impressions except those to which it had been long and exclusively accustomed.[5]

5. In order to give more force to this assertion, it may be observed, that, in proportion as man advances beyond the period of his infancy, the exercise of his senses becomes, every day, less universal. In the first stage of his life, he wishes to see everything, and to touch every thing; he puts to his mouth every thing that is given him; the least noise makes him start: his senses are directed to all objects, even to those which have no apparent connection with his wants. In proportion to his advancement beyond the stage of infancy, during which is carried on, what may be called the *apprenticeship* of the senses, objects strike him only so far as they happen to be connected with his appetites, his habits, or his inclinations. Afterwards it is often found, that there is only one or two of his senses which awaken his attention. He becomes, perhaps, a musician, who, attentive to every thing that he hears, is indifferent to every thing which he sees. Perhaps he may turn out a mere mineralogist, or a botanist, the first of whom, in a field fertile in objects of research, can see nothing but minerals; and the second, only vegetable productions. Or he may become a mathematician without ears, who will be apt to say, after having been witness to the performance of one of the tragedies of Racine; '*what is it that all this proves?*' If, then, after the first years of infancy, the attention is naturally directed only to those objects which have some known and perceived connection with our tastes, the reason may be easily conceived why our young savage, feeling only a small number of wants, was induced to exercise his senses only on a small number of objects. This, if I mistake not, was the cause of that perfect inattention which struck every body on his first arrival at Paris; but which, at the present moment, hath almost altogether disappeared, evidently because he has been made to feel his connection and dependence upon all the new objects which surround him.

It may be easily conceived, then, why the ear, though very apt to perceive certain noises, may yet be very little able to discriminate the articulation of sounds. Besides, in order to speak, it is not sufficient to perceive the sound of the voice; it is equally necessary to ascertain the articulation of that sound: two operations which are very distinct, and which require the organ to be in very different conditions. For the first, there is need only of a certain degree of sensibility in the nerve of the ear; the second requires a particular modification of that sensibility. It appears possible, then, that those who have ears well organized, and duly sensible, may still be unable to seize the articulation of words. There are found, among cretins, a great number of persons who are dumb and yet not deaf. Among the pupils of Citizen Sicard there are several children who hear perfectly well the sound of a clock; a clapping of hands; the lowest tones of a flute or violin, and who, notwithstanding, have never yet been able to imitate the pronunciation of a single word, even when loudly and slowly articulated. Thus, it appears, that speech is a kind of music to which certain ears, although well organized in other respects, may be insensible. The question is, whether this be the case of the child that we are speaking of? I do not think it is, although my favourable opinion rests on a scanty number of facts. It is true that my experiments, with a view to the ascertaining of this point, have not been numerous, and that I was for so long a time embarrassed with regard to the mode of conduct that I ought to pursue, that I restricted myself to the character of an observer. What follows are the result of my observations.

During the four or five first months of his residence at Paris, the Savage of Aveyron appeared sensible only to those particular sounds to which I have already alluded. In the course of the month Frimaire he appeared to understand the human voice, and, when in the gallery that led to his chamber, two persons were conversing, in a high tone, he often went to the door, in order to be sure if it was properly secured; and he was so attentive as to put his finger on the latch to be still farther satisfied. Some time afterwards, I remarked that he distinguished the voice of the deaf and dumb, or rather, the guttural sound which continually escapes them in their amusements. He seemed even to be able to ascertain the place whence the sound came; for, if he heard it whilst he was going down the stair-case, he never failed to re-ascend, or to descend more precipitately, according as the noise came from below or above.

At the beginning of the month Nivose, I made a remark still more interesting. One day whilst he was in the kitchen, busy in boiling potatoes, two persons, behind him, were disputing with great warmth, without his appearing to pay the least attention to them. A third came in, who joining in the discussion, began all his replies with these words: '*Oh! it is different.*' I remarked, that every time this person permitted his favourite exclamation to escape him, 'Oh!' the Savage of Aveyron suddenly turned his head. I made, in the evening, about the hour of his going to bed, some experiments with regard to this particular sound, and I derived from them very nearly the same results. I tried all the other vowels without any success. This preference for *o* induced me to give him a name, which, according to the French pronunciation, terminates in that vowel. I made choice of that of *Victor*. This name he continues to have, and when it is spoken in a loud voice, he seldom fails to turn his head, or to run to me. It is, probably, for the same reason, that he has since understood the meaning of the negative monosyllable *no*, which I often make use of, when I wish to make him correct the blunders which he is now and then guilty of in our little exercises and amusements.

Whilst these developments of the organ of hearing were going on, in a slow but perceptible manner, the voice continued mute, and was unable to utter those articulate sounds which the ear appeared to distinguish; at the same time the vocal organs did not exhibit, in their exterior conformation, any mark of imperfection; nor was there any reason to suspect it in their interior structure. It is true that there was observable, on the upper and anterior part of the neck, a scar of considerable extent, which might excite some doubt with regard to the soundness of the subjacent parts, if the suspicion were not done away by the appearance of the scar. It seems in reality to be a wound made by some cutting instrument; but, by observing its superficial appearance, I should be inclined to believe that it did not reach deeper than the integuments, and that it was united by what surgeons call the *first intention*. It is to be presumed that a hand more disposed than adapted to acts of cruelty, wished to make an attempt upon the life of this child; and that, left for dead in the woods, he owed, to the timely succour of nature, the speedy cure of his wound; which could not have been so readily effected, if the muscular and cartilaginous parts, belonging to the organ of voice, had been divided.

This consideration leads me to think, that when the ear began to perceive some certain sounds, if the voice did not repeat them, it was not on that account fair to infer any organic lesion; but that we ought to ascribe the fact to the influence of unfavourable circumstances. The total disuse of exercise renders our organs inapt for their functions; and if those already formed are so powerfully affected by this inaction, what will be the case with those, which are growing and developing without the assistance of any agent that was calculated to call them into action? Eighteen months at least are necessary, of a careful and assiduous education, before a child can lisp a few words: have we then a right to expect, that a rude inhabitant of the forest, who has been in society only fourteen or fifteen months, five or six of which he has passed among the deaf and dumb, should have already acquired the faculty of articulate speech! Not only is such a thing impossible, but it will require, in order to arrive at this important point of his education, much more time, and much more labour, than is necessary to children in general. This child knows nothing; but he possesses, in an eminent degree, the susceptibility of learning every thing: an innate propensity to imitation; an excessive flexibility and sensibility of all the organs; a perpetual motion of the tongue; a consistence almost gelatinous of the larynx: in one word, every thing concurs to aid the production of that kind of articulate and almost indescribable utterance, which may be regarded as the involuntary apprenticeship of the voice: this is still farther assisted by occasional coughing and sneezing, the crying of children, and even their tears, those tears which we should consider as the marks of a lively excitability, but likewise as a powerful stimulus, continually applied, and especially at the times most seasonable for the simultaneous development of the organs of respiration, voice, and speech. Let these advantages be allowed me, and I will answer for the result. If it be granted me, that we ought no longer to depend on the youth of Victor; that we should allow him also the fostering resources of nature, which is able to create new methods of education, when accidental causes have deprived her of those which she had originally planned. At least I can produce some facts which may justify this hope.

I stated, at the beginning of this section, that it was my intention to lead him to the use of speech. Being convinced, by the considerations thrown out in these two last paragraphs, and by another not less conclusive, which I shall very soon explain, that it was necessary only to excite, by degrees, the action of the larynx, by the allurement of objects necessary to his wants. I had reason to believe that the vowel *o* was the first understood; and I thought it very fortunate for my plan, that this simple pronunciation was, at least in sound, the sign of one of the wants most frequently felt by this child. However, I could not derive any actual advantage from this favourable coincidence. In vain, even at those moments when his thirst was most intolerable, did I frequently exclaim *eau, eau*, bringing before him a glass of water: I then gave the vessel to a person who was near him, upon his pronouncing the same word; and regained it for myself by this expression: the poor child tormented himself in all kinds of ways; betrayed a desire for the water by the motion of his arms; uttered a kind of hissing, but no articulate sound. It would have been inhuman to have insisted any longer on the point. I changed the subject, without, however, changing my method. My next endeavours were with regard to the word *lait*. The fourth day of this my second experiment, I succeeded to the utmost of my wishes; I heard Victor pronounce distinctly, in a manner, it must be confessed, rather harsh, the word *lait*, which he repeated almost incessantly: it was the first time that an articulate sound had escaped his lips, and of course I did not hear it without the most lively satisfaction. I nevertheless made afterwards an observation, which deducted very much from the advantage which it was reasonable to expect from the first instance of success. It was not till the moment, when, despairing of a happy result, I had actually poured the milk into the cup which he presented to me, the word *lait* escaped him again, with evident demonstrations of joy; and it was not till after I had poured it out a second time, by way of reward, that he repeated the expression. It is evident from hence, that the result of the experiment was far from accomplishing my intentions; the word pronounced, instead of being the sign of a want, it appeared, from the time in which it was articulated, to be merely an exclamation of joy. If this word had been uttered before the thing that he desired had been granted, my object would have been nearly accomplished: then the true use of speech would have been soon acquired by Victor; a point of communication would have been established between him and me, and the most rapid progress must necessarily have ensued. Instead of this, I had obtained only an expression of the pleasure which he felt, insignificant as it related to himself, and useless to us both. In fact, it was merely a vocal sign of the possession of a thing. But this, I repeat it, did not establish any communication between us; it could not be considered as of any great importance, as it was not subservient to the wants of the individual, and was subject to a great number of misapplications, in consequence of the daily-changing sentiment of which it was become the sign. The subsequent results of this misuse of the word have been such, as I feared would follow: it was generally only during the enjoyment of the thing, that the word *lait* was pronounced. Sometimes he happened to utter it before, and at other times a little after, but always without having any view in the use of it. I do not attach any more importance to his spontaneous repetition of it, when he happens to wake during the course of the night.

After this result, I totally renounced the method by which I obtained it, waiting for a time when local circumstances will permit me to substitute another in its place, which I think will be more efficacious. I have abandoned the organ of voice to the influence of imitation, which, although weak, is not, however, altogether extinct, as appears from some little advancements that he has since made.

The word *lait* has served Victor as the root of two other mono-syllables, *la* and *li*, to which he attaches certainly still less meaning; he has since a little modified the last, by adding to it a second *l*, pronouncing both together like the *gli* of the Italian language. We frequently hear him repeat *lli*, *lli*, with an inflexion of voice which is not altogether destitute of melody. It is astonishing that the liquid *l*, which, with children in general, is one of the most difficult sounds to articulate, is yet one of the first that he hath distinctly pronounced. I should not, perhaps, be far from the truth in believing, that this remarkable circumstance arises from a kind of inclination that he feels for the name of Julia, a young lady between eleven and twelve years of age, who has lately been passing some weeks with Madame Guérin, her mother. It is certain at least that, since the exclamations *lli*, *lli*, have become more frequent, and, according to the report of his gouvernante, are heard even during the night, at those moments when there is reason to believe that he is in a profound sleep, it is impossible accurately to ascertain the cause, and the precise nature and importance of this last fact; we must wait till a more advanced puberty hath furnished us with a greater number of observations. The last acquisition of the organ of his voice is a little more considerable, and consists of two syllables, which, in fact, are well worth three, in consequence of the manner in which he pronounces the last; it is the exclamation, *Oh Dieu!* which he has learnt from Madame Guérin; he frequently permits it to escape him in his occasional fits of excessive joy: in pronouncing it, he suppresses the *u* of the word *Dieu*, and dwells on the *i*, as if it were doubled, so that he may be heard distinctly to cry out, *Oh Diie! Oh Diie!* the *o* in this last combination of sound was not new to him, as I had some time before succeeded in enabling him to pronounce it.

Let us now see, so far as the organ of voice is concerned, the exact point at which we have arrived. We may observe, that all the vowels, except the *u*, already enter into the small number of the sounds which he articulates, and that there are only three consonants among them, viz. *l*, *d*, and *l* liquid. This progress is, no doubt, very small, if it be compared to that degree of advancement which is necessary to the complete development of the human voice; but it has appeared to me sufficient to demonstrate the possibility of this development. I have spoken above of the causes which must necessarily render it a long and difficult process; there is still another which will likewise contribute to retard his improvement in articulate utterance, which I ought not to pass over in silence. I allude to the facility which our young savage shews in expressing in other ways, than by speech, the small number of his wants:[6] all his wishes are expressed by the most unequivocal signs, which, in a certain sense, have, like ours, their gradations and synonimes. When the hour for walking is arrived, he presents himself repeatedly before the window and the door of his chamber. If he then perceives that his gouvernante is not ready, he lays before her, in order, all the articles necessary to her toilet, and often, in his impatience, he even sets about assisting to dress her. This done, he goes down the stairs first, and himself takes hold of the latch of the door. When arrived at the observatory, the first thing is to ask for some milk; this he does by presenting a wooden bowl, which he never forgets, on going away, to put into his pocket; with this he first provided himself, the day after having broken, in the same house, a china cup which used to answer the same purpose.

Again, in order to render complete the pleasure of his excursions, we have for some time past indulged him with the amusement of being carried about in a wheel-barrow. Since then, whenever he is seized with a desire for it, if nobody is present to oblige him, he goes again into the house, lays hold of some one by the arm, leads him into the garden, and puts into his hands the arms of the barrow;

6. My observations afford additional confirmation to the important opinion of Condillac, who observes, in speaking of the origin of the language of sounds, the language of action, then so natural, was a great obstacle to be surmounted. Was it likely that this should be abandoned for another, the advantages of which could not be foreseen, and the difficulty of which was so strongly felt?

if this invitation be neglected, he himself takes hold of the handles, wheels it a few paces, and places himself again in it, imagining, without doubt, that, if his desires are not gratified after all this, it is not for the want of having clearly manifested them.

Is he impatient to dine? his intentions are still less equivocally expressed; he himself lays the cloth upon the table, and presents to Madame Guérin the plates, that she may go into the kitchen to fill them. When he dines with me in town, all his wishes are expressed to the lady who does the honours of the table. It is always to her that he addresses himself to be served with what he wants. If she pretend not to understand him, he puts his plate by the side of the dish of which he desires to partake, and devours it with his eyes. If this do not produce any effect, he takes a fork and strikes it two or three times on the edge of the dish. If she still neglect him, he loses all patience; he plunges a spoon or even his hand into the dish, and, in the twinkling of an eye, he empties it all into his own plate. He is no less expressive in the manner of exhibiting the affection of his mind, and especially impatience and ennui. A great number of the curious know how, with more natural frankness than politeness, he dismissed them, when fatigued with the length of their visits; he presents to each of them, and yet without a countenance of contempt, their cane, gloves and hat, pushes them gently towards the door, which afterwards he violently shuts upon them.[7]

In order to complete the history of this pantomimic language, it is necessary that I should farther add, that Victor understands it with as much facility as he speaks it: if Madame Guérin wishes to send him for some water, she need only shew him the pitcher, and make him see that it is empty, by inverting the vessel. An analogous proceeding is all that is sufficient for me, in order to get him to serve

7. It is worthy of remark, that this language of action is entirely natural to him; and that, during the first days of his entrance into society, he employed it in the manner most expressive. 'When he felt thirst,' said Citizen Constans St Esteve, who had seen him in the beginning of this interesting period, 'he cast his eyes on the right and left; having perceived a pitcher, he put my hand into his own, and led me towards it, and then struck it with his left hand, in order to denote his wish to drink; I carried him some wine, which he disdained to take, expressing impatience at my delay in giving him some water instead.

me with something to drink, when we dine together, or at any other time. But what is still more astonishing in his readiness in these means of communication, is, that there is no need of any preliminary lesson, in order to make him understand them. I satisfied myself of this one day by an experiment of the most conclusive nature; I chose, from amongst a multitude of others, a thing for which I was previously assured that there did not exist between him and his gouvernante any indicating sign; such was, for example, the comb, which was kept for his purpose, and which I wished him to bring to me. I should have been much mistaken, if, by disordering my hair with my hand, and shewing him my head in this state, I had not been understood.

Many persons see, in all these proceedings, only the common instinctive actions of an animal; as for myself, I confess, that I recognize in them the *language of action*, in all its simplicity; that primitive language of the human species, originally employed in the infancy of society, before the labour of many ages had arranged and established the system of speech, and furnished to civilized man a fertile and sublime means of indefinite improvement, which calls forth his understanding even in his cradle, and of which he makes use all his life without appreciating what he is by means of it, and what he would be without its assistance if he were accidentally deprived of it, as in the case which at present occupies our attention. Without doubt a day will arrive, when more multiplied wants will make our young Victor feel the necessity of using new signs. The defective use which he has made of his first sounds, will, of necessity, much retard the approach of this epoch, but will not prevent its ultimate arrival. It will be the same thing, neither more nor less, than what happens to the child who at first lisps the word papa, without attaching to it any idea, goes on saying it, in all places, and on all occasions, then addresses it to every man that he sees; and it is not till after a multitude of reasonings, and even abstractions, that he is able to make an exclusive and just application of it.

SECTION V. My fifth object was *to exercise, during some time, on those things which were connected with his physical wants, the most simple operations of his understanding; and afterwards to direct the application of them to matters of instruction.*

Contemplated in the earliest stage of his infancy, and in regard to his understanding, man appears not as yet elevated above other animals. All his intellectual faculties are rigorously circumscribed within the narrow sphere of his physical wants. It is to them alone that the operations of his understanding are directed. It behoves us then, in education, to make use of these wants for his instruction; that is to say, to a new order of things which have no original connection with them. From this application flow all his knowledge, all the improvement of his mind, and even the conceptions of the most sublime genius. Whatever degree of probability there may be in this idea, I bring it forward here again, only as it is the point of departure from the line of conduct which I have hitherto pursued.

I shall not enter minutely into a detail of the means that were made use of, in order to exercise the intellectual faculties of the Savage of Aveyron, with regard to the objects of his appetites. These means consisted simply in placing between him and his wants, obstacles that are continually increasing, and continually changing in their nature, and which he could not surmount without perpetually exercising his attention, his memory, his judgment, and all the functions of his senses.[8] Thus were developed all the faculties

8. It is not improper to remark, that I have not experienced any difficulty in my first aim. Whenever his wants are concerned, his attention, his memory, and his intelligence seemed to raise him above himself; it is a remark that might have been made on every trial, and which, if it had been duly reflected upon, would have led us to anticipate the most successful result. I do not scruple to say, that I regard, as a great proof of intelligence, his having been able to learn, at the end of six weeks residence in society, to prepare his food, with all the care and attention to minutiae, of which Citizen Bonaterre has given us an account. 'His occupation, during his stay at Rodez,' says this naturalist, 'consisted in shelling kidney beans; and he executed this task with as great a degree of discernment, as could have been shewn by a person who was the most habituated to the employment. As he knew, by experience, that these vegetables were destined for his subsistence, as soon as a bunch of dried pods were brought him, he used to go for a kettle, and establish the scene of this operation in the middle of his apartment. There he arranged his materials in the most commodious manner possible. The pot was placed on

which might be subservient to his instruction; and now we had nothing more to do than to find out the most easy means of turning them to account.

As yet little progress has been made with regard to the sense of hearing, in this respect, the Savage of Aveyron was merely upon a level with one of the deaf and dumb. This consideration induced me to try the method of instruction which has been adopted by Citizen Sicard. I began by the first steps usual in that celebrated school, and drew, upon a black board, the lineal figure of certain objects, which a simple design was sufficient to represent; such as a key, scissors, and a hammer. I repeatedly placed, at those moments when I saw that I was observed, each of the objects; and when I was satisfied by this, of his having perceived the relations that they bore to each other, I wished him to bring me them in succession, making by my finger the figure of that which I asked for. I obtained nothing by this; I returned to the experiment a great many times, and always with as little success: he either refused, from obstinacy, to bring me that of the three things that I marked out, or with this he brought the two others, and presented them all to me at the same time. I was myself convinced that this was merely to be attributed to his indolence, by which he was prevented from doing, at different times, what he perceived might as well be done at once. I then thought it right to make use of a method which forced him to direct his attention to each of these objects separately. I had observed, even for some months past, that he had a remarkable taste for order; it was on this account that he sometimes got out of his bed in order to arrange any piece of furniture or utensil which happened to be out of its proper place. This propensity still more decidedly shewed itself with regard to those things which were suspended on the wall; each

---

his right hand, and the beans on his left; he opened the shells one after the other with an inimitable suppleness of fingers; he put into the kettle the good grains, and threw away those which were unfit for use; if, by chance, any grain escaped him, he took it up and placed it with the others. As he emptied the shells, he piled them beside him in exact order, and when his work was finished, he took up the kettle, and after having filled it with water, placed in on the fire, the heat of which he increased by means of the empty shells, which he had put in a separate heap.

had its particular nail and hook; and when any change was made in their situation, he was not at rest 'till he replaced them himself. I had then only to arrange, in the same manner, the things on which I wished to exercise his attention. I suspended, by a nail, each of the objects below the figure which represented them, and left them for some time. When afterwards I took them away, and gave them to Victor, they were immediately replaced in their proper order. I recommenced the experiment a great many times, and always with the same result: I was far, however, from attributing it to his discernment; this classification might simply be an act of the memory. In order to satisfy myself with regard to this point, I changed the respective position of the figures, and I then saw him, without any regard to this transposition, arrange the objects in the same order as before. In fact nothing was so easy as to teach him the new classification forced upon him by this new change, but nothing more difficult than to make him reason with regard to it. His memory had all the merit of each arrangement. I then contrived to deprive him, in some measure, of the assistance which he drew from this source. This I did by continually fatiguing his memory, by increasing the number of figures, and with the frequency of their inversions. In that case the faculty of recollection would become an insufficient guide for the methodical arrangement of all these numerous bodies, and therefore the understanding must have recourse to a comparison of the design with the thing. What an important point should I then have achieved! Of this I had no longer doubt, when I saw young Victor attach his looks in succession to each of the objects, to choose one of them, and then to seek the figure to which it belonged; and of this I had very soon a more substantial proof, by trying the inversion of the figures, which was followed, on his part, by the inversion of the objects themselves.

This circumstance inspired me with the most flattering hopes; I thought I should not have any more difficulties to overcome, when one presented itself of an insurmountable nature, which obstinately arrested me in my progress, and forced me altogether to renounce my method of proceeding. It is well known that, in the instruction of the deaf and dumb, this first step of comparison is commonly succeeded by a second, which is much more difficult. After having taught, by repeated comparisons, the relation which the thing bears to the design, they place behind the latter all the letters which form the name of the object represented by the figure. This done, they efface the figure, and there remain only the alphabetical signs. The pupil in the school of the deaf and dumb perceives, in this second step, only a change of design, which to him still continues the sign of the object. It was not the same with Victor, who, notwithstanding the most frequent repetitions, notwithstanding the protracted exhibition of the thing below the name belonging to it, could never know the thing by the word. It took me no time to account for this difficulty; it was easy to understand why it was insurmountable. Between the figure of an object, and its alphabetical representation, the distance is immense, and so much the greater to the pupil, as it presents itself to him at the very threshold of instruction. If the deaf and dumb are not arrested by it in the progress of their improvement, the reason is, that they, of all children, are the most attentive, and the most observing. Accustomed from their earliest infancy to understand and to speak by the eyes, they are, more than any other persons, exercised in perceiving the mutual relations of visible objects.

On these accounts it was then necessary to look out for some method more suitable to the faculties scarcely developed of our young savage. It was with this view that I formed my new plan of proceeding: I will not stop to make an analysis of it; the reader will judge of it by the execution.

I pasted, on a board of two feet square, three pieces of paper of a very distinct form, and a very decided difference of colour: there was one circular and red; another triangular and blue; and the third square and black. Three pieces of pasteboard, of the same colour and figure, were, by means of a hole pierced in the middle of them, and nails properly arranged on the board, placed and left for some days on their respective models. Having afterwards taken them away and presented them to Victor, they were replaced by him without any difficulty. I found, by inverting the board, and by that means changing the order of the figures, that this first result of my experiment was not merely a matter of routine, but was the consequence of comparison. After some days I substituted another board in the place of the first: I there represented the same figures, but they were all of an uniform colour. In the first, the pupil was assisted in his comparison both by the forms and the colours: in the second, he had no other guide than the observation of the forms. Almost immediately afterwards I presented a third board to him, on which all the figures were equal, but the colours different; the same trials were always followed by the same results. I pay little regard to a few accidental negligences of attention. The facility with which these comparisons were formed induced me to present new ones to him. I made additions and variations in the two last tables. I added to that of the figures, other forms much less distinct, and to that of the colours, new colours, which had only a slight shade of difference between them. There was, for example, in the first, a parallelogram by the side of a square; and in the second, a pattern of celestial blue by the side of one of a grey blue. This gave rise to some blunders and perplexities, but they disappeared after a few days exercise.

These happy results emboldened me to try new changes, gradually increasing in difficulty; each day I added, I retrenched, I modified, and induced the necessity of new comparisons and of new judgments. At length the multiplicity and numberless complications of these little exercises altogether exhausted his attention and docility. Then re-appeared, in all their intensity, those emotions of impatience and of fury which burst out so violently during the first weeks of his residence at Paris, whenever he was unexpectedly imprisoned in his chamber. This did not signify; it seemed to me that the moment was arrived when it behoved me no longer to appease these emotions by complaisance, but to endeavour to overcome them by decision. I then thought it my duty to persist. Thus, for instance, when being disgusted with a task, of which in fact he did not conceive the object, and with which of course it was very natural he should be fatigued; he took it into his head to seize the pieces of pasteboard, to throw them indignantly on the ground, and to run to his bed in a fury. I permitted him to pass one or two minutes quietly. I then returned to the business with the most perfect indifference: I made him gather up all the pieces of pasteboard which were scattered in his chamber; and gave him no respite until they were replaced in their proper order. My perseverance lasted only a few days; for it was at length overcome by the unconquerable independence of his spirit. His emotions of anger became more frequent, more violent, and resembled the paroxysms of rage similar to those of which I have already spoken; but with this striking difference, that the effects of his passion were now less directed towards persons than things. He would, when he was in this humour, gnaw the bed-clothes, even the mantle-piece, throwing about in his chamber the fire-irons, the cinders, and the burning coals, and conclude the scene by falling into convulsions, which seemed to be of a nature somewhat analogous to those of epilepsy, a complete suspension of the sensorial functions. I was obliged to yield when things had arrived at this pitch: and yet my acquiescence had no other effect than to increase the evil; its paroxysms became more frequent, and liable to be renewed by the least opposition, often even without any evident cause.

My embarrassment now became extreme. I perceived myself, at the moment when all my assiduities had succeeded only so far as to convert this poor child into an unfortunate epileptic, repeated attacks, and the force of habit, confirmed a malady, which is one of the most terrible, and least curable, in the catalogue of human diseases. It behoved me then as soon as possible to remedy it, not by medicines, which are so often ineffectual, not by gentleness, from which there was no longer any reason to expect advantage, but by a treatment that was calculated to awaken horror, very nearly similar to that which Boerhaave had employed in the hospital at Harlem. I was perfectly convinced that if the first method which I was about to adopt, should fail of its effect, that the evil would only be exasperated, and that every mode of treatment of a similar nature would become ineffectual. In this firm conviction I made choice of that which I believed would be most alarming to a being, who as yet did not know, in his new state of existence, any species of danger.

Some time before, Madam Guérin being with him at the observatory, the platform of which is very much elevated from the ground: as soon as he approached near the parapet, he was seized with terror, and an universal trembling; his face was covered with moisture; he drew her by the arm towards the door, and did not recover himself till he had reached the bottom of the stairs: what might be the cause of his terror is a thing that I was not anxious to ascertain; it was sufficient for me to know the effect of it, in order to make it subservient to the execution of my purpose. An opportunity very soon presented itself: during a most violent fit of passion, which I had reason to believe was excited by the repetition of our exercises, taking advantage then of the moment when the functions of the senses were not as yet suspended, I suddenly opened the window of the chamber, which was on the fourth storey, looking down upon a rough pavement. I approached him with every appearance of fury, and seizing him forcibly, I held him out of the window, his face directly turned towards the bottom of this precipice; when, after some seconds, I withdrew him from this situation, he appeared pale, covered with a cold sweat; his eyes moistened with tears, and still agitated with a slight trembling, which I attributed to the effects of fear: I then took him again to his boards; I made him gather up his scattered papers, and insisted that they should be all replaced. All this was executed, although, it must be confessed, in a slow and rather slovenly manner. He did not, however, venture to betray any impatience. After it was done, he threw himself on his bed, and burst into a flood of tears.

This was the first time, at least to the best of my knowledge, that he shed tears. The circumstance of which I have already given an account; I mean, the occasion on which the remorse that he felt in having quitted his gouvernante, or the pleasure of finding her again, excited tears, was posterior to the time of which I am speaking. If I have represented it as previous in my narration, the reason is, that in my plan I have attended less to chronological order, than to the methodical development of facts.

This singular method was followed by a degree of success, which, if it was not complete, was at least satisfactory. If his disgust for labour was not entirely surmounted, at least it was much diminished, without ever producing effects similar to those of which we have been just giving an account. On those occasions, when he was fatigued a little too much, or when he was compelled to devote to labour those hours which were usually set apart for his excursions or his repast, he went no farther than to express, *ennui*, impatience, and to utter a plaintive murmur, which in general terminated in a flood of tears.

This favourable change permitted us to re-assume the course of our exercises, in which I made new modifications, that appeared to me still better calculated to fix his attention and to improve his judgment. I substituted, instead of the figures pasted on boards, and which were, as I already said, entire plans, representing geometrical figures, some designs which were merely outlines of these same plans. I contented myself also with marking the colours by small patches of an irregular form, and by no means analogous in their conformation to the coloured pieces of pasteboard. The new difficulties were only an amusement for the child, a result which was quite sufficient to serve the purpose which I had in view, in adopting this system of gross comparisons. The moment was now arrived of substituting it for another, more instructive, and which would have presented insurmountable difficulties, if they had not been previously done away by the success of the means which we have employed in order to surmount the former.

I printed, in large characters, on some pieces of pasteboard, two inches square, the twenty-four letters of the alphabet. I cut in a board an equal number of squares, in which I inserted the pieces of pasteboard, without, however, fastening them to it, in order that I might be able to change their places at pleasure. An equal number of alphabetic characters were cast in metal; these letters were intended to be compared, by the pupil, with the printed letters, and classed in their corresponding squares. The first attempt to ascertain the efficacy of this method, was made, in my absence, by Madame Guérin: I was much surprised to learn from her, on my return, that Victor distinguished all the characters, and classed them in a proper manner. He was put to the trial immediately, and he performed his task without committing the least error. Delighted with such rapid success, I was, however, far from being able to explain the cause of it; and it was not, till some days afterwards, that it appeared to me to arise from the manner in which our pupil proceeded to this classification. In order to render it more easy to him, he thought of a little expedient, which freed him in this task from exercising either memory, comparison, or judgment. When the board was put into his hands, he did not wait till we took the metallic letters from their squares; he withdrew them himself, and piled them in his hand, according to the order of their classification; so that the last letter of the alphabet was found, after the board was completely stripped, to be the uppermost of the pile. It was with this that he commenced, and with the last of the pile that he finished; beginning at the end of the board, and invariably proceeding from right to left. This is not all; this employment was susceptible of improvement; for sometimes the pile in his hand would fall down, and the characters be disarranged; then it was necessary to put them in order, merely by the efforts of attention. The twenty-four letters were placed in four ranks, six in each; it was then more simple to remove them by their ranks, and to replace them in the same manner, so as not to proceed to the stripping of the second pile till the first was re-established.

I do not know if he reasoned about it; but it is certain that he executed the thing in the way that I represented. It was a routine, but a routine that required invention, and which did as much honour to his intelligence, as a methodological classification did to his discernment. It was easy to put him in this tract, by giving the characters in a state of disorder every time that the board was presented to him. In short, in spite of the frequent inversions that I made, notwithstanding certain insidious arrangements of these characters, such as placing the G beside the C, the E beside the F, etc., his discernment was not to be disturbed. In exercising him with all these characters, my object was to prepare Victor for making them subservient to their primitive use; that is to say, to the expression of wants which may be manifested by speech. Far from imagining that I was so near this grand epoch of his education, it was a spirit of curiosity, rather than a hope of success, which suggested to me the following experiment:

One morning, as he was impatiently waiting for the milk, I arranged on a board, which I had the evening before prepared expressly for the purpose, these four letters, L. A. I. T. Madame Guérin, whom I had previously instructed, approaches, looks on the characters, and gives me afterwards a bowl full of milk, which I pretended was for my own use. Almost immediately afterwards I went up to Victor; I gave him the four letters which I had taken from the board; I pointed to the board with one hand, whilst with the other I presented him with a vessel full of milk. The letters were immediately replaced, but in an inverted order; so that the word which they formed was TIAL, instead of LAIT. I then marked out the corrections necessary to be made, by pointing with my finger to the letters which were to be transposed, and the place that he ought to give to each; when these changes had reproduced the sign of the thing, I made him wait no longer for it.

It will be scarcely credited, that five or six similar trials were sufficient not merely to teach him the way of arranging methodically the four letters *lait*, but also, I may say, to give him an idea of the relation that there was between this alphabetical arrangement, and one of his wants; that is to say, between the word and the thing. This, at least, I have a decided right to infer, from what occurred eight days after this first experiment. He was seen, just before his evening excursion to the observatory, to provide himself, of his own accord, with the four letters in question; to put them in his pocket, and immediately on his arrival at the house of Citizen Lemeri, where, as I said before, he went every day to take milk, to produce these letters on a table, in such a manner as to form the word *lait*.

It was originally my intention to have recapitulated here all the facts that are scattered through this work; but I have since thought that whatever force they might acquire by their re-union, it would not equal that which arises from this last result. I therefore give it to the public unconnected with any reflections, in order that it may mark, in a manner still more striking, the epoch at which we are already arrived, and become a security for that which it is reasonable for us to expect that we shall ultimately reach. In the meantime we have a right to conclude, from our observations, especially from those which have been recorded in these two last sections, that the child known under the name of the Savage of Aveyron, is endowed with the free exercise of all his senses; that he gives continual proofs of attention, reflection, and memory; that he is able to compare, discern, and judge, and apply in short all the faculties of his understanding to the objects which are connected with his instruction. It is proper to remark, as a point of essential importance, that these happy changes have been produced in the short space of nine months, and in a subject which was supposed to be incapable of attention; hence we are authorised in concluding, that his education is possible, if it is not even absolutely demonstrated already by these early instances of success, independently of those that we may in future expect from time, which, in its invariable progress, seems gradually to bestow upon infancy those powers, intellectual and moral, which it insensibly steals from man on the decline of life.[9]

9. It is in the power of enlightened observers to come and satisfy themselves of the accuracy of these results; they alone are capable of appreciating the proper value of these facts, by bringing with them, to the investigation, an understanding that is judicious, and versed in the science of the human mind. The exact moral state of our savage, it is difficult to ascertain with precision; daily experience, and all our received ideas are calculated to mislead our judgment with regard to this subject. '*If the habit in which we are,*' says Condillac, speaking of a similar case of being assisted by signs, '*would permit us to remark every thing which we owe to them, we should have nothing to do, but to place ourselves in the situation of this young man, in order to understand the reason why he was so slow in acquiring knowledge; but the fact is, that we always draw our inferences from our own circumstances.*' It is likewise necessary, in order to form a sound judgment, in the case of this child, not to be satisfied with a single examination, but to observe it and study it repeatedly; at every moment of its excursions, during every one of its amusements, in the midst of its little exercises; all this is absolutely necessary. They are not even sufficient, if, in order to form an exact comparison between the present and the past, we have not seen with our own eyes, the Savage of Aveyron during the first months of his residence at Paris. Those who have not observed him at that period, and

In the meantime, it may be desirable to state some of the most important inferences relative to the philosophical and natural history of man, that may be already deduced from this first series of observations! Let them be collected; let them be classed with method; let them be reduced to their exact value, and we shall see in them a material proof of the most important truths; of those truths, for the discovery of which Locke and Condillac were indebted merely to the force of their genius, and the depth of their reflections. It seems to me, at least, that the following conclusions may be drawn:

1. That man is inferior to a great number of animals in a pure state of nature,[10] a state of vacuity and barbarism, although it has been unjustly painted in colours the most attractive; a state in which the individual, deprived of the characteristic faculties of his species, drags on miserably, equally without intelligence and without affections, a life that is every moment subject to danger, and confined to the bare functions of animal nature.

2. The next conclusion that may be drawn is, that moral superiority which has been said to be *natural* to man, is merely the result of civilization, which raises him above other animals by a great and powerful stimulus. This stimulus is the predominant sensibility of his species; the essential property from which flow the faculties of imitation, and that unintermitting propensity which forces him to seek, in new wants, new sensations.

3. It may be observed, that this imitative power, adapted for the education of all his organs, and especially for the acquisition of

---

who see him at the present instant, would perceive in him only a child, that is nearly like other children, except that he does not speak; they could not be duly sensible of the important distance which exists between this being and the Savage of Aveyron, just after he had been introduced into society, at a distance, in appearance, trifling, but in fact immense, when we properly reflect upon it, and calculate through what a series of new reasons and acquired ideas he must have gone in order to have arrived at these last results.

10. I have not the least doubt, that, if we were to insulate, at the earliest period of infancy, two children, the one male and the other female, and were to do the same with two quadrupeds, chosen from the species of brutes, that was the least intelligent, these latter would not shew themselves much superior to the former, in the means of providing for their wants, and in taking care either of their own preservation, or that of their children.

speech, although very energetic and active during the first years of life, is rapidly enfeebled by the progress of age, insulation, and all the other causes which tend to deaden the nervous sensibility. From whence it results that the articulation of sounds, which is beyond contradiction of all the effects of imitation, the most inconceivable and advantageous result, cannot fail to experience innumerable obstacles at an age which has not advanced beyond the period of infancy.

4. We may likewise remark, that there exists equally with the savage the most insulated, as with the citizen raised to the highest point of civilization, a uniform proportion between their ideas and their wants; that their continually increasing multiplicity, in a state of polished society, ought to be regarded as one of the grand instruments for producing the development of the human mind; so that we may be allowed to lay it down as a general proposition, that all the causes, whether accidental, local, or political, which tend to augment or diminish the number of our wants, contribute of necessity to extend or to contract the sphere of our knowledge, and the empire of the sciences, of the fine arts, and of social industry.

5. The last observation that we shall make on the present subject is, that in the actual state of our physiological knowledge, the progress of teaching may, and ought to be aided by the lights of modern medicine, which of all the natural sciences can co-operate the most effectually towards the amelioration of the human species, by appreciating the organical and intellectual peculiarities of each individual; and by that means determining what education is likely to do for him, and what society may expect from his future character.

There still remain some considerations of no trifling importance, which I had intended to have annexed to those that have been already stated; but the illustrations which they would have required would have trespassed the limits, and been inconsistent with the design of this little work. I moreover perceived, in comparing my own observations with the doctrines of some of our metaphysicians, that I dissented from them on certain interesting points. I ought of course to wait for a greater number of facts, from which I may be able to draw a more certain and secure conclusion. A motive very similar to the preceding has prevented me, when speaking of all the developments of young Victor's constitution, from dwelling upon the period of his puberty, which has shewn itself, for some *decades* past, in a most striking and unequivocal manner; and the first appearances of which cast considerable suspicion on the origin of certain affections of the heart, which we regard as very *natural*. I ought not, at this stage of my investigation, to be precipitate in judging and in drawing conclusions. I am deeply impressed with the persuasion, that until they are matured by time, and confirmed by farther observations, that we ought to refrain from publishing, or even entertaining speculations, which may have a tendency to destroy prejudices in themselves perhaps respectable, and which, beyond all doubt, constitute the most amiable, as well as the most consoling illusions of social life.

Report on the Progress of Victor of Aveyron

(*1806, printed 1807*)

FOREWORD

To his Excellency the Minister of the Interior

My Lord,

To speak to you of the Wild Boy of Aveyron is to remind you of a name which now arouses no interest; it is to recall a being forgotten by those who saw him for but a moment and despised by those who thought to judge him. For my part, I have been his careful witness and mentor, always indifferent to the forgetfulness of some and the disdain of others; the evidence of five years of daily observation permits me to present to Your Excellency the report you await, to recount what I have seen and what I have done, to describe the present condition of this young man, the long and difficult paths he has trodden, the obstacles he has overcome as well as those he has failed to surmount. If these details, my lord, seem too insignificant for your attention and well below your expectations, then I beg you to believe that if I had not received from you a formal request for this report, I would gladly have enveloped in a profound silence and condemned to eternal oblivion an undertaking whose outcome offers less a story of the pupil's progress than an account of the teacher's failure. But let me judge myself impartially: if you disregard my original aim and view the enterprise in a more general light, my lord, I think you will see with some satisfaction that the experiments I have tried and the observations I have made have produced a collection of facts relevant to the illumination of the history of medical philosophy, the study of uncivilized man and the organization of certain types of private education.

To understand the present state of the Wild Boy of Aveyron, you must recall his past condition. If we are to judge this young man properly, we must compare him only with himself.

Beside a youth of the same age, he is only an unfortunate creature, an outcast of nature and of society. But within the simple comparison of Victor as he was and Victor as he is, one cannot but marvel at the vast gulf which lies between them and indeed there is more difference between our present Victor and the Wild Boy of Aveyron than between the same boy and other individuals of his present age and kind.

I will not distract you, my lord, with the dreadful picture of the man-animal as he was when he left his wild forests. I described him then in a small work which appeared a few years ago and which I now have the honour to present to you and I showed him as he was described by a famous doctor speaking to a learned society. I will recall only that after a long examination and many efforts the commission represented by this doctor was unable to capture this child's attention and sought in vain to discern in his actions and his wishes some act of intelligence or some evidence of sensibility. A stranger to the reflective process which is the mainspring of our ideas, he fixed his attention on no single object, because no object made any durable impression on his mind. His eyes looked but did not see, his ears heard but did not listen, and the organs of touch, limited to the mechanical operation of seizing and holding, had never been used to verify the shape or the existence of any object. Such was the state of the moral and physical faculties of this child that he found himself not only in the lowest rank of his species, but also among the lowest of the animal kind, and one could indeed say that he differed from the plant only in that he had the ability to move and to shout. Between this less than animal existence and the present condition of Victor, there is a prodigious difference which appears even more striking if I restrict myself to a close comparison of the two extremes, ignoring the intervening progress. But convinced that to contrast these two pictures is less valuable than to give a true and faithful account of what has happened, I shall try my utmost to describe the changes which have taken place in the condition of this young creature and for the sake of order and general progress I shall recount the appropriate facts in three separate sections, each relating to the triple development of the functions of the senses, the intellect and the emotions.

DEVELOPMENT OF THE FUNCTIONS OF THE SENSES

I. It is the works of Locke and Condillac which have shown the powerful influence exercised by the isolated and simultaneous action of the senses on the formation and development of our ideas. The abuse made of this discovery has destroyed neither its truth nor its practical applications to a system of medical education. These were the principles I began to follow after I had fulfilled the principal aims already described in my first work, setting myself to exercise and develop each of Victor's sense organs in turn.

II. Since of all the senses hearing is the one which contributes most particularly to the development of our intellectual faculties, I began to use every possible resource to awake our young savage's ears from their long torpor. It seemed to me that to educate this sense I would have to find some means of isolating it and as Victor's entire system had only the smallest amount of sensibility, I was obliged to concentrate it on the sense I wished to develop, artificially paralysing that of sight, the sense wherein the greatest sensitivity lies. Consequently, I covered Victor's eyes with a thick blindfold and I subjected his ears to the loudest and most dissimilar sounds. My plan was not only to make him hear them, but to make him listen. To obtain this result, as soon as I had made a sound I made Victor produce another like it by striking the same sonorous object and then strike a different one as soon as his ear warned him that I had changed my instrument. My first endeavours sought to make him distinguish between the sound of a bell and that of a drum, and as one year previously I had been able to lead Victor from the simple comparison of two pieces of card variously coloured and illustrated to the distinction of letters and words, I had every reason to believe

that the ear, following the same development of attention as that of
the eye, would soon come to distinguish the most similar as well as
the most disparate tones of the vocal organ or of speech. I therefore
set myself to produce sounds which were progressively less dissimilar, more complicated and nearer together. Soon, I was not
satisfied with Victor's simply distinguishing between the sound of a
drum and the sound of a bell and I required him to note the difference in sound produced by the drumstick striking either the skin
or the metal frame or the body of the drum, or the bell of a clock,
or a fire shovel.

III. I next adapted this comparative method to the perception of
the notes of a wind instrument, more nearly analogous to those of
the voice, the last stage in my plan for leading my pupil towards the
appreciation of the different intonations of the larynx. My expectations were rewarded and as soon as the sound of my voice fell upon
his ears, I found him sensible to the faintest change of intonation.

IV. In these last experiments, I could not as previously require
my pupil to repeat the sounds he perceived. By dividing his attention, this double task would have been outside the plan I had drawn
up, namely to educate each of his senses separately. I therefore
restricted myself to requiring the simple perception of sounds. To
achieve this, I placed my pupil in front of me, eyes blindfold, hands
clasped, and I made him point a finger every time I uttered a sound.
This means of testing was quickly understood; hardly had he heard
my voice than he raised his finger with a sort of impetuosity and
often with an outburst of delight, which left me in no doubt as to
whether he enjoyed these curious lessons. In fact, whether he took
genuine pleasure in the sound of the human voice or whether he had
at last overcome the ennui of being deprived of light for hours on
end, he many times came to me in the period between the lessons,
blindfold in hand, and placing it over his eyes, positively trembled
with pleasure when he felt my hands tying it firmly behind his head.
It was however only in these latter experiments that I noted such
evidences of delight. At first, I congratulated myself, and far from
repressing them, positively encouraged their occurrence, little

thinking that I was preparing for myself an obstacle which was soon to interrupt this series of useful experiments and annul the results so arduously acquired.

v. After assuring myself by means of the experiments previously described that Victor could perceive all vocal sounds whatever their degree of intensity, I applied myself to the task of making him compare them. It was now no longer a question of merely counting the sounds of the voice, but of appreciating their differences and noting the modifications and varieties of tone which compose the music of speech. Between this task and the preceding one lay a vast gulf for a creature whose development depended on gradual effort and who could progress towards civilization only because I led him gently and imperceptibly along the way. When I approached this difficult task, I armed myself more than ever with patience and gentleness, encouraged in addition by the hope that once this obstacle was overcome, the sense of hearing would be much improved. We began by comparing the vowels, and once more the hand was used for the performance of the experiment. Each of the five fingers represented one of the vowels and was to be raised when the vowel had been perceived. Thus the thumb represented A and was to be raised when this vowel was pronounced; the index finger was the sign of E, the middle finger I and so on.

vi. It was only with difficulty and much effort that I managed to give him a clear idea of the vowels. The first one he clearly distinguished was O; next came A. The three others offered greater difficulties and for a long time were totally confused: in time however the ear began to distinguish between them and it was then that the outbursts of delight I have already mentioned began to appear afresh. However, our new experiments demanded from my pupil greater attention, delicate comparisons and repeated judgements and it so happened that these outbursts of pleasure which had hitherto done no more than brighten our lessons now disrupted them completely. The sounds would be totally confused, the fingers raised indiscriminately, often all at once, with wild impetuosity and irritating bursts of laughter. To repress this unwelcome gaiety, I decided to restore my pupil's freedom of vision and carry on with the lessons with a severe and even threatening face. There was no more laughter, but instead a continual distraction of the sense of hearing, since the eyes were now eagerly engaged on an examination of all the surrounding objects. The least alteration in the arrangement of furniture or clothing, the slightest movement from the people around him, a sudden change in sunlight, everything attracted his attention, everything was a reason for a change of place.

I replaced the blindfold on his eyes and the laughter began again. I then began to threaten him with actions since my looks could no longer contain him. I armed myself with one of our drumsticks and tapped him on the fingers every time he made a mistake. He took this punishment for a joke and his pleasure increased accordingly. To disabuse him, I decided to make his punishment more severe. I was understood, but it was not without a mixture of pain and pleasure that I saw from the boy's saddened face how he felt the pain of the blow far less than the feeling of injury. Tears rolled down beneath his blindfold; I hastened to remove it; but whether from distress or fear, or some inner preoccupation of his senses, he kept his eyes tight shut. I cannot describe how unhappy he looked with his eyelids closed and tears coursing down his cheeks. At this moment as at many times before, I was only too ready to abandon my self-imposed task, acknowledge as wasted the time I had spent, ready to wish that I had never known this child and to condemn the heartless and vain curiosity of those men who had wrenched him away from a life of happy innocence.

VII. This scene ended the noisy gaiety of my pupil. However, I had no reason to congratulate myself for my success and I had overcome one problem only to have to face another. A feeling of fear took the place of his wild delight and our exercises were even more difficult than before. As soon as I had uttered a sound, I would have to wait for over a quarter of an hour for the agreed signal; and even when it was correct, it came with slowness and such deep uncertainty that if by chance I made the slightest sound or movement, the startled child would quickly put down his finger for fear of being mistaken and with the same slowness and circumspection would raise another. I still did not despair and felt certain that time, gentleness and encouragement would dissipate this unfortunate and excessive timidity. Vain hopes – everything was useless. Thus I saw the end of the brilliant hopes I had founded, not without reason, on an uninterrupted chain of useful and interesting experiments. Since that moment, I have tried the same tests many times and have always been forced to abandon them by the same obstacle.

VIII. Nevertheless, this series of experiments on the sense of hearing was not totally useless. Victor owes to it the ability to hear clearly many single-syllable words and to distinguish very carefully between different intonations of speech and pick out those relating to reproach, anger, sadness, scorn and friendship, even when these different emotions are not accompanied by any appropriate facial movements or by such natural gestures as usually attend them.

IX. Saddened rather than discouraged by the lack of success achieved with the sense of hearing, I determined to devote all my efforts to the sense of sight. My first endeavours had already much improved it and had so contributed to his powers of concentration that at the time of my first report he could already recognize metal letters and arrange them in such a way as to form various words. There was still a considerable distance between this point and the clear perception of written characters and the mechanism of writing, but happily these difficulties were all of the same order and were easily overcome. Within a few months, my pupil could read and write quite passably a series of words sufficiently similar in appearance for an inattentive eye to misjudge them. It was however an intuitive reading: Victor read the words without pronouncing them and without knowing their meaning. Though this method of reading, the only one practicable for a child like Victor, may not be worthy of great attention, one might still wonder how I could be sure that words which were not pronounced and which for him had no meaning at all could be read sufficiently accurately for him to avoid confusion. There is nothing simpler than the method I used to achieve this certainty. All the words used in the experiment were written on two boards; I held one of these and gave the other to Victor; then with the tip of the finger I touched each word on the board in turn and required Victor to show me its equivalent on his board. I took care to follow a different order of arrangement on each board so that no word appeared in exactly the same place. This made it essential for Victor to study carefully the appearance of each word in turn in order to identify it at a glance.

x. When my pupil was misled by the appearance of a word and indicated some other in its place, I made him correct his mistake not by indicating he was wrong but by making him instantly spell out the word. Spelling for him was mentally comparing one after the other all the letters forming the two words in question. This genuinely analytical examination was very swift: with a pointer, I would touch the first letter of the other word; then we would move to the second letter and so on until Victor, seeking in his word the letters I showed him in mine, would come upon that letter which allowed him to recognize the difference between the two words.

xi. It was soon unnecessary for us to use such a detailed method for him to recognize his mistakes. It was enough for me to make him look carefully for a moment at the word he mistook for another for him to appreciate the difference; and the mistake was corrected as soon as it was indicated. In this way we exercised and perfected this important sense whose meaningless mobility had caused the failure of the first attempts to capture and hold it and had given rise to the first suspicions of idiocy.

xii. My education of the sense of sight being at an end, I turned my attention to that of touch. Though I did not share the opinion of Buffon and Condillac on the importance of this particular sense, I did not regard as wasted the attention I proposed to give to the touch or as without interest the observations I might make as to its development. My first memoir showed that this sense, originally restricted to the mechanical actions of taking and holding, had improved its faculties through the effect of hot baths, notably the faculty of perceiving heat and cold and the roughness and smoothness of objects. However, if one considers the nature of these two types of sensation, it will be seen that they are both related to the skin which covers our entire body. The organ of touch which had received its share of the general sensitivity I had awakened in the cutaneous system had until that moment functioned as it were only as part of that system, since it did not differ from it in any special way.

XIII. My first experiments confirmed this view. At the bottom of an opaque vase whose mouth was just big enough to permit the entry of a hand, I placed some cooked chestnuts which were still hot and some raw, cold chestnuts of approximately the same size. One of Victor's hands was inside the vase and the other lay open on his lap. I placed a hot chestnut on this open hand and told Victor to pick a similar one out of the vase. This he did. Then I gave him a cold chestnut and the one he withdrew from the case was exactly similar. I repeated the experiment several times and always with the same success. The result was different however when instead of asking him to compare the temperature of these items I wished him to judge their shape by the same means. Here the exclusive functions of touch truly begin and this sense was totally new. I placed chestnuts and acorns in the vase and when I wanted Victor to produce from the bottom of it the equivalent of what I held in my hand, he would bring an acorn for a chestnut and a chestnut for an acorn. This sense then had to be trained to function in exactly the same way as the other senses. I therefore required Victor to compare shapes and forms very different from each other, both in shape and in size, such as a stone and a chestnut, a coin and a key. It was not easy for him to distinguish the one from the other by touch alone. As soon as he learnt to identify them, I replaced them with other less dissimilar objects, such as an apple, a nut and some small pebbles. Then I had him examine chestnuts and acorns in the same exploratory way and by this time the test was no more than an easy game for my pupil. I reached the point where he could recognize metal letters by touch alone, even such similar ones as B and R, I and J, C and G.

xiv. As I said earlier, I was not too hopeful of success in this particular type of exercise, but in the event it made a useful contribution to the sensibility of my pupil; later, I saw his frail intelligence struggle to overcome much more serious difficulties, but I never saw his face take on that serious, calm and thoughtful air but when he contemplated the difference in shape of objects submitted to this tactile examination.

xv. There remained for my attention the senses of taste and smell. The latter was so delicate that it defied improvement. For a long time after his arrival in Paris, our young savage retained the habit of smelling everything given to him, even objects which seem to us odourless. When we walked in the country during his first months in the city, I often saw him stop, even retrace his steps in order to pick up pebbles and bits of dried wood which he would throw away only after smelling them carefully and often with every appearance of deep satisfaction. One evening he lost himself in the Rue d'Enfer and was not found by his gouvernante till nightfall; it was only after sniffing her hands and arms over and over again that he decided to go home with her and allowed himself to show the joy he felt at seeing her again. Civilization could add nothing to the delicacy of his sense of smell. Linked as it is more to the exercise of the digestive functions than to the development of the intellectual faculties, it lay somewhat outside the scope of my plan of study. It would seem perhaps that the sense of taste, being related to the same functions, would be equally foreign to my purpose. I did not consider the matter in this light, however, believing that taste plays a greater role than the limited function assigned to it by nature in that it relates to pleasures as varied as they are numerous – a gift of civilization – and it seemed to me advantageous to develop, or rather, pervert it. I think it of no real purpose to list here all the expedients I used for this end and by means of which I succeeded in awakening the taste of our young man for a whole quantity of dishes he had hitherto always disdained. In the midst of these newly acquired pleasures, Victor showed none of the greedy preferences which constitute gluttony. Unlike those men we term savages who live in a state of semi-civilization and who have learnt all the vices of society without acquiring any of its virtues, Victor grew accustomed to new food whilst remaining indifferent to strong drink. This indifference changed to aversion following an incident the effect and circumstances of which perhaps deserve to be recounted. Victor was dining with me in town. At the end of the meal, he served himself from a carafe which contained extremely strong spirits and which, having neither colour nor smell, looked exactly like water. Our wild boy took it for water and poured himself half a glass; suddenly thirsty, he swallowed more than half before the burning sensation in his stomach warned him of his mistake. Throwing aside both glass and contents, he leapt to his feet and with a bound was in the doorway, howling and running backwards and forwards along the corridors and staircase of the house, always on the same path, like a wounded animal seeking not, as the poets say, to avoid the arrow that pursues but rather to assuage his pain by constant movement, a relief he could not beg by word of mouth.

XVI. Meanwhile in spite of this aversion for spirits, Victor has grown to like wine, though he does not seem to miss it particularly when he is not given any. I would go so far as to say that he has always kept a distinct preference for water. The way he drinks it seems to suggest that it is one of his greatest pleasures, but this doubtless relates to some cause other than pure enjoyment. Almost always at the end of dinner, even when he is no longer very thirsty, we see him like a gourmet before a glass of some exquisite liqueur – he fills his glass with pure water, takes a sip and swallows it drop by drop. What adds interest to this scene is its setting. He drinks his water standing at the window, eyes turned towards the countryside as if in this moment of sheer delight this child of nature seeks to unite the only two things which remain from his lost freedom, a drink of clear water and the sight of the sun on the countryside.

XVII. In this way the senses were improved. Apart from hearing, every sense awoke and opened up new perceptions and carried into the mind of our young savage ideas as yet undreamt of. But these ideas left in his brain but a faint and fleeting trace and to fix them there it was necessary to impress on his mind their respective signs, or better still, the value of those signs. Victor knew them already because I had always combined the perception of objects and their tangible qualities with the reading of the words which represented them, without however trying to convey their meaning. Victor, taught to distinguish by touch a round object from a flat one; by sight a red paper from a white one; by taste a sour liquid from a sweet one, had at the same time learnt to distinguish the names which expressed these different perceptions, but without being able to recognize the representative value of these signs. This knowledge no longer belonged to the domain of the external senses and therefore came within the scope of the mental faculties. Passing beyond the realm of the external senses, this knowledge fell finally within the domain of the faculties of the mind and it became necessary to ask Victor, if one may put it thus, to describe the ideas brought to him by these senses. This became the object of a new set of experiments which form the subject of the following section.

DEVELOPMENT OF THE INTELLECTUAL FUNCTIONS

XVIII. Although presented separately, the facts composing the previous section are linked in many ways with those which are to form the subject of the study to come. For, my lord, such is the close connection between physical man and intellectual man that even though their respective fields appear and in fact are very distinct, the dividing line between the two is blurred and difficult to find. Their development is simultaneous and their influence reciprocal. Thus, whilst I was restricting my efforts to the development of the senses of our wild boy, the mind took its share of the attention given to the education of these organs and followed the same order of development. It seems that by teaching the senses to perceive and distinguish new objects, I was forcing the attention to fix itself upon them, the powers of judgement to compare them and the memory to retain them. In these exercises, everything was of value; everything passed into the mind; everything brought into

play the faculties of the intelligence and prepared them for the great
task of the communication of ideas. I knew already that this was
possible by training my pupil to indicate his needs by means of
letters arranged so as to give the name of the thing he desired. I
have already described in my first report how he took his first step
in the recognition of written signs and I was not afraid to claim this
as a most important stage in his education, the sweetest and most
brilliant success ever obtained from a creature fallen, as this one
was, into the lowest state of brutishness. Later observations, however, threw light on the true meaning of this success and weakened
my expectations. I had familiarized Victor with certain words so
that he could express his needs and desires by indicating them and I
noticed that far from using them for this purpose, he reserved them
for certain moments only and always used them at the sight of the
desired object. Thus, for example, however much he wanted milk, it
was only when he usually drank it and at the very instant he saw it was
about to be given to him that the word for this food was spoken, or
rather formed in the appropriate way. This circumstance aroused my
suspicions and in order to allay them, I delayed the hour of his meal
and I waited in vain for my pupil to express his needs, though these
became exceedingly urgent. It was only when the cup appeared that
the word *lait* was formed. I tried another test: in the middle of his
meal and without giving the action any appearance of a punishment
I took away the cup containing the milk and locked it in a cupboard. If the word *lait* had been for Victor the distinct sign of the
object and the expression of the need he felt for it, I cannot doubt
but that after this sudden deprivation and with the continued need
for the object the word *lait* should have been produced. It did not
appear and I concluded that the formation of this sign, instead of
being the expression of my pupil's needs, was no more than a sort
of preliminary exercise, a mechanical process which preceded the
satisfaction of his appetites. It was therefore essential to retrace our
steps and start afresh. I resigned myself courageously, convinced
that if I had not been understood by my pupil then the fault was
mine rather than his. In fact, when I reflected upon the causes

which could have given rise to this faulty acceptance of written signs, I realized that I had not used in these first examples of the expression of ideas the same simplicity I had used in my other methods of instruction and which indeed had ensured my success. Thus, though the word *lait* is for us no more than one simple sign, for Victor it must be a confused expression for many things, the drink itself, the vessel containing it and the desire of which it was the object.

XIX. Many other signs I had made familiar to him showed the same lack of preciseness in their application. An even worse defect was apparent in our method of expression. As I have already said, this consisted of arranging a series of metal letters on the same line and in a proper order in such a way as to give the name of each object. But the relationship which exists between the word and the object was not so immediate as to be completely understood by the pupil. To remove this difficulty, it was necessary to establish between the object and its sign a more direct liaison and a sort of identity which would fix themselves simultaneously in his memory; moreover, it was necessary that the first objects used for this new method of expression should be reduced to the greatest simplicity so that their signs could in no way bear upon their accessories. Following this plan, I placed on the shelves of a bookcase a few simple objects such as a pen, a key, a knife, a box and so on, each on a card bearing its name. None of the names was new to my pupil; he knew them already and had learned to distinguish them from each other by the method of reading I have already described.

XX. What remained was to familiarize his eyes with the apposition of the word and its appropriate object. He quickly understood what I was about and I had the proof of this when I changed the places of the objects and put the labels in a different order: Victor carefully replaced each object on its proper label. I varied my tests; and this diversity allowed me to make various observations relating to the degree of impression made by the image of the written signs on our wild boy's sensory apparatus. I placed all the objects in one corner and the labels in another, requiring Victor to go in search of the object whose name appeared on the card; I found that if he were to bring me this object he could not lose from sight for a single moment the characters used to indicate it. If he was too far away to read the label or if I covered it with my hand after he had looked at it closely, the image of the word instantly escaped him and with an anxious, worried air he would bring me the first thing that came to hand.

XXI. The result of this experiment was not encouraging and would indeed have discouraged me completely if I had not noticed that after frequent repetition the impression of the word on my pupil's mind began to last much longer. Soon he had barely to glance at the card I showed him in order to go and find the appropriate object without haste and without mistake. After a time, I extended the experiment by sending him from my room to his bedroom to find and return with the object whose name I showed him. The duration of the perception was at first much shorter than the duration of the journey; but by an act of intelligence worthy of note Victor sought and found in the agility of his legs a sure means of making the impression last longer than his swift journey from room to room. As soon as he had read the label, he shot away like an arrow and returned a moment later with the object in his hand. Sometimes, though, the memory of the word would escape him and I would hear him stop in his tracks and return to my room with a timid and worried air. Sometimes he had only to cast his eyes on the whole collection of words to recognize and remember the one he had forgotten; at other times the image of the word had so far escaped his memory that I had to show him the card again: indeed he would ask me to do this by taking my hand and moving my index finger over the whole collection of words till I pointed out the one he had forgotten.

XXII. This exercise was followed by another which by offering more work to his memory contributed largely to its development. Until then, I had asked for only one object at a time; I next asked him for two, then three, and then four, indicating an equal number of words to my pupil who, sensing the difficulty of remembering them

all, ran his eyes over them eagerly till I hid them from his gaze. There
was neither delay nor uncertainty. He hastened to his room and
brought back the objects I had asked for. On his return, his first
care before giving them to me was to look once more at the list, to
compare it with the objects he carried and to keep it with him until
he had made sure by this means that there was neither omission nor
mistake. At first, this experiment gave varying results, but the
difficulties it presented were finally overcome. The pupil, now sure
of his memory, scorned the advantage offered him by the agility of
his legs and carried out the exercise slowly and calmly, often stopping in the corridor, looking out of the window which is at one end
of it and greeting with loud cries the splendid view of the countryside there visible; and then he would set off again for his room, take
up his small cargo, repeat his act of homage to the still-regretted
beauties of nature and enter my room in the sure certainty of making
no mistake.

XXIII. In this way, the memory was restored to its full functions
and succeeded in retaining the symbols of thought whilst at the
same time the intelligence perceived their full meaning. This at least
was what I concluded from the preceding facts, when I saw Victor
use, either during our exercises or quite spontaneously at other
times, the different words whose meanings I had taught him, or ask
for the various things they represented, showing us or giving us the
object when the word was given him to read, or indicating the
word when he was shown the object. Surely one must accept that
this double test was more than sufficient to assure me that I had
finally reached the end to achieve which I had had to retrace my
steps and make so great a detour? What happened next made me
think for a moment that I was farther from it than ever.

XXIV. One day when I had taken Victor into my apartment and
was about to send him to his bedroom as usual to find various
objects in his list of words, I took it into my head to lock my door
and take the key out of the lock without his noticing. This done, I
went back into my study where he was waiting and unrolling his
list I asked for some of the objects named thereon, taking care not

to indicate any which were not also in my apartment. He set off instantly; but finding the door locked and having sought unsuccessfully for the key he came to me, took my hand and led me to the entrance door as if to show me that it could not be opened. I feigned surprise and pretended to look for the key, and even to try and open the door by force; finally, abandoning these vain attempts, I took Victor back into my study and showing him the same words again, invited him by signs to look around the study and see if some similar objects could be found there. The words indicated were stick, bellows, brush, glass, knife. All of them were scattered around the room, but in positions where they were easy to see. Victor saw them and touched none of them. I had no greater success in making him recognize them when I gathered them together on a table and it proved useless to ask for them one after the other by showing him all their names in turn. I tried another method; I cut out with scissors the names of these objects and thus transformed into labels they were placed in Victor's hands; thus returning to our first steps in this experiment, I required him to place on each object the word which served to indicate it. It was in vain; and I experienced the inexpressible chagrin of seeing my pupil fail to recognize any of these objects, or rather the relationships which linked them to their signs, and with an air of indescribable stupefaction move his uncomprehending eyes over these characters, all once again suddenly meaningless to him. I felt my heart sink with impatience and discouragement.

I went and sat down at the far end of the room and considered bitterly this unfortunate creature whose strange condition reduced him to such sad alternatives: he could either be sent to one of our asylums as a downright idiot or spend his life striving to achieve an education which would hardly serve to increase his happiness. 'Unhappy creature,' I said with a sad heart, as though he could hear me, 'since my labours are wasted and your efforts fruitless, go back to your forests and the wild life of yore; or if your new needs now leave you dependent on a society which you cannot serve, then go and die of poverty and boredom at Bicêtre.' Had I not known the limitations of his intelligence, I could have believed myself fully understood; for barely had I uttered these words than I saw an expression of great sorrow on his face, his chest heaved with sobs, his eyes closed and tears streamed down his cheeks.

xxv. I had often noticed that similar emotions, when they went so far as tears, produced a most salutary crisis and led to a sudden development of intelligence, making it possible for hitherto un-surmountable difficulties to be swiftly overcome. I had also noticed that if, at the height of this passion, I changed from reproaches to caresses and a few words of friendship and encouragement, I would produce a flood of emotion which doubled the effort I was expect-ing. This was a favourable moment and I hastened to profit from it. I went across to Victor; I spoke to him affectionately and in terms he could understand, and offered him clear marks of my love and friendship. His tears flowed more freely, accompanied by sobs and sighs, I showed myself even more attentive and with demonstrations of affection took his emotion to the highest point till, if I might put it thus, the last fibre of his moral being trembled. When this excitement had subsided, I replaced the same objects before his eyes and invited him to point them out to me, one after the other, as I showed him their names. I began by asking him for the book; he looked at it for a long time, made as if to touch it, whilst looking into my eyes for a sign of approval or disapproval which could calm his uncertainty. I took care to keep my face expressionless. Thus reduced to his own judgement, he decided that this was not the desired object and his eyes wandered all around the room, pausing only at the books which were scattered on the table and the mantel-piece. This review of the room was a flash of illumination to me. I instantly opened a cupboard which was full of books, and took out a dozen, taking care to include among them one which was exactly like the book Victor had left in his room. To see it, take it in his hand and give it to me was the work of a moment for Victor.

xxvi. I took this test no further. The result was sufficient to renew the hopes I had too lightly abandoned and to enlighten me on the difficulties caused by the experiment. It was clear that my pupil, far from having conceived a false idea of the signs, had merely applied to them a too strict interpretation. He had obeyed my instructions to the letter; and as I had limited myself to giving him the names of things in his room, he had assumed that these objects were the only ones to which the names were applicable. Thus a book which was not the one in his room was not a book for Victor; and if it were to have the same name, then it was necessary that a perfect resemblance should establish a visible identity between the two. Insofar as this concerns the application of words, it is far different from the practice of children who when they learn to speak give individual names the value of generic names but within the restricted meaning of the individual names. What could have caused this curious difference? Unless I am mistaken, it arose from a keenness of visual observation, a necessary result of the special education given to his sense of sight. I had exercised this organ of sense so thoroughly in the recognition of the visible qualities of objects and their differences of dimension, colour and shape, that when he considered two identical objects his skilled eyes could always find enough points of dissimilarity for him to consider them essentially different. Having determined the source of the mistake, it was easy to remedy it; it was to establish the identity of objects by showing my pupil the identity of their uses and their properties; it was to make him see the common qualities which impart the same name to things which seem different in appearance. In a word, it was a matter of teaching him to consider objects not from the point of view of their difference, but according to their similarity.

XXVII. This new study was a kind of introduction to the art of comparison. My pupil devoted himself to it so completely that he went astray once more by attaching the same idea and giving the same name to objects which had no connection between them other than some similarity of shape or use. Thus he gave the name book indiscriminately to a handful of paper, a notebook, a newspaper, a pamphlet; every long thin piece of wood was a stick, a brush might be a broom, or a broom a brush, and soon, if I had not overcome this confusion of similarities, I would have seen Victor limit himself to a small number of signs which he would have applied indiscriminately to a mass of different objects whose only common link was some general quality or property.

XXVIII. In the midst of these mistakes, or rather these oscillations of an intelligence always more asleep than awake and constantly stirred by artificial means, I thought I perceived one of the faculties typical of man, particularly thinking man, namely the faculty of invention. By considering things from the point of view of their similarity or of their common properties, Victor concluded that since many objects enjoyed a resemblance of shape they must also have in certain circumstances an identity of use and function. Doubtless the conclusion was rather risky, but it gave rise to judgements which even when they were clearly faulty became for him so many more means of instruction. I remember one day when I asked him in writing to bring me a knife, he searched for some time then contented himself with bringing me a razor which he went to fetch from a room next door. I pretended to be satisfied with it and when his lesson was over and I gave him his tea as usual, I insisted that he cut his bread instead of breaking it with his fingers as he usually did. To this end, I offered him the razor he had given me under the name of knife. He acted consistently and tried to use it as a knife, but the instability of the blade prevented him. I did not consider the lesson complete; I took the razor and put it to its proper use in Victor's presence. Henceforward, in his eyes this instrument was no longer and could never be a knife. I took his notebook and showed him the word *knife* and my pupil instantly showed me the one he held in his hand, which I had given him when he found he could not use the razor. To complete the experiment, I had to effect the counter-proof: if I gave him the notebook and touched the razor, he should react by touching no word in the list, for he did not know the name of this object: this is in fact exactly what happened.

XXIX. At other times, the substitutions he made were suggestive of much stranger comparisons. I remember that we were dining in town one day when someone offered him a helping of lentils at a moment when there were no clean plates available; he took it into his head to take down from the mantelpiece and hold out as he would a plate a small circular picture under glass, surrounded by a frame whose smooth projecting edge was not unlike that of a plate.

xxx. But often his experiments were far happier, more successful in every way, and deserving the name of invention. I do not fear to use this term in connection with the way he one day provided himself with a pencil-holder. Once only, in my study, I made him use such a device to hold a piece of chalk too small to be comfortable in his fingers. A few days later, the same difficulty arose; but this time Victor was in his room and there was no pencil-holder available for his chalk. I ask the most industrious or inventive man among us to guess or even to do what Victor did to provide himself with one. He found a utensil used in roasting meat in most good kitchens, though hardly ever used by a poor creature like himself, a skewer to be exact, but a rusty old one long forgotten in a cupboard. This was the instrument he chose to replace the one he lacked and which, in a burst of truly creative imagination, he transformed into a real pencil-holder by substituting a few twists of thread for the usual sliding device. You will excuse the importance I place on this act, my lord. One must have suffered all the pains and anxieties of this long instruction, one must have followed and guided this vegetable-creature in his arduous development from the first moment of attention to this first spark of imagination before one can appreciate the joy I felt; you must forgive the pride I feel at so ordinary and simple a feat. What added even more importance to the event, considered as a proof of progress and a promise of future improvement, was that instead of occurring in isolation and therefore accidentally, it was one incident among a crowd of others, less interesting in themselves, but which since they occurred at the same time and came from the same source, suggested the varied results of a general impulse. It is indeed worthy of note that this moment saw the spontaneous disappearance of a great number of routine habits which my pupil had contracted whilst attending to the daily tasks prescribed for him. Whilst avoiding any forced comparisons or drawing false conclusions, one can at least suspect, I think, that this new way of looking at things, which suggested the idea of putting them to new purposes, must necessarily have forced the boy to step outside the restricted circle of his more or less automatic habits.

XXXI. Convinced at last that I had established in Victor's mind the link between objects and their signs, it only remained for me to increase their number gradually. If the process by which I succeeded in establishing the meaning of the first signs has been properly understood, it will be clearly seen that this procedure would be applied only to a limited number of objects of small size for one cannot label a bed, a room, a tree, a person nor constituent parts inseparable from a whole. I had no difficulty in conveying to him the meaning of these new words, though I could not link them visibly to the objects they represented as I had in previous experiments. To be understood, I had only to point at the new word and indicate with the other hand the object to which the word referred. I had some difficulty in conveying to him the nomenclature of the parts which make up a whole. Thus the words fingers, hands, forearm had no clear meaning for my pupil for quite a time. This confusion in the attribution of signs evidently arose from the fact that he had not yet understood that the parts of the body, considered separately, were distinct objects with particular names of their own. To convey this idea to him, I took a bound book, tore off the covers and pulled out several pages. As I gave Victor each part, I wrote its name on the blackboard; then taking the various parts from his hands, I made him show me the appropriate words. When they were firmly fixed in his memory, I put these separated parts together again, and, asking him their name once more, was answered as before; then without giving him any particular part and showing him the book in its entirety, I asked him its name; he pointed to the word book.

XXXII. It was now a simple matter to make him familiar with the nomenclature of the different parts of compound bodies; and so that he should not confuse the names of the parts with the general name of the whole, I took care in my demonstrations to touch the individual parts, but when I came to the general name, I would only indicate the object vaguely and did not touch it.

XXXIII. From this demonstration, I passed to the properties of bodies and here I entered the realm of abstractions. I entered it with the fear of not being able to pass beyond the threshold and of finding myself halted by unsurmountable difficulties. There were none; and my first demonstration was instantly understood, even though it related to one of the most abstract concepts, that of size. I took two books of identical bindings but of different size; one was an octodecimo and the other an octavo. I touched the first. Victor opened his notebook and pointed to the word book. I touched the second; my pupil pointed to the same word. I repeated this several times, always with the same result. Next I took the smaller book and passing it to Victor, I made him place his hand flat on the cover; it was almost big enough to hide the book completely. Then I made him do the same thing with the octavo volume; his hand barely covered half of it. So that he should not misunderstand my intention, I indicated to him the part still uncovered and made him stretch out his fingers towards it; he could do this only by uncovering a portion equal to the one he was covering. After this experiment which demonstrated the difference of size in so tangible a manner, I asked him the name once more. Victor hesitated: he felt that the same word could no longer be applied to two objects he had found to be of different sizes. This was what I was waiting for. I wrote the word *book* on two cards and placed one on each book. I next wrote *big* on a third card and *small* on a fourth; I placed them alongside the first cards, one on the octodecimo volume and the other on the octavo. After drawing Victor's attention to this arrangement, I picked up the labels, shuffled them together for a moment and gave them back to Victor to place on the books. He performed the task correctly.

XXXIV. Had I been understood? Had he seized the respective meanings of *big* and *small*? To have sure and certain proof, this is what I did: I took two nails of different length; I compared them more or less as I had the books. Then having written the word *nail* on two cards, I gave them to Victor without adding the adjectives *big* or *small*, hoping that if he had understood the previous lesson he would apply to the nails the same signs of relative size as he had used to establish the dimensions of the books. He did as I had hoped so quickly that the proof now seemed to me conclusive. This was the process I used to teach him the concept of size. I used it with equal success to teach him the signs representing other sensible properties of objects such as colour, weight, strength, etc.

XXXV. After the explanation of the adjective came the verb. To make my pupil understand it, I had only to submit to various operations an object whose name he knew already, indicating to him at the same time the infinitive of the verb describing the action. I took a key, for example; I wrote its name on the blackboard; then *touching* it, *throwing* it, *picking* it up, *carrying* it to the lips, *replacing* it, etc., I wrote the verb at the same time as I performed the action, and put down in a list alongside the word *key* the verbs to *touch*, to *throw*, to *pick up*, to *kiss*, to *replace*, etc. Then I substituted for the word *key* some other object which I treated in a similar way, at the same time pointing at the verbs already written. It often happened that when I replaced one object with another in order to associate it with the same list of verbs, such an incompatibility arose between the verbs and the new object that the action requested became bizarre or impossible. My pupil's consequent confusion served to his advantage as well as to my satisfaction since it provided him with the opportunity of exercising his discernment and myself with further proofs of his intelligence. One day, for instance, a series of changes in the objects produced such strange associations as *tear stone*, *cut cup*, *eat broom*; he found a way out of the confusion by changing the two actions indicated by the first two verbs for two other verbs more compatible with the objects. Thus he took a hammer to break the stone, and dropped the cup to break it. When he came to the third verb and could find no suitable replacement, he decided to change the object, so he took a piece of bread and ate it.

XXXVI. Reduced as we were to long and laborious efforts in our study of grammar, we worked at the same time – as a means of further instruction as well as an indispensable diversion – on the exercise of writing. The beginnings of this work offered innumerable difficulties which indeed I had expected. Writing is an exercise in imitation and imitation had yet to appear in our savage. Thus, when I first gave him a piece of chalk and set it comfortably in his fingers, I could obtain from him no line or stroke which might suggest that my pupil had any intention of imitating what he saw me doing. Here too we had to return to first principles and seek to rouse his imitative faculties from their inertia by submitting them, like all the others, to a sort of gradual education. I put this plan into execution by making Victor practise such simple acts of imitation as raising his arms, lifting his foot, sitting down and standing up exactly as and when I did; then we moved on to opening the hand, clenching it and repeating with the fingers a host of movements I performed for him, simple at first and then more elaborate. Next I put into his hand and mine a long pointed stick which I made him hold like a quill pen with the two-fold intention of giving more strength and skill to his fingers through the difficulty of keeping this imitation pen properly balanced, and at the same time of showing him the slightest movements of the stick in a way both clear and capable of imitation.

XXXVII. Our preliminary exercises over, we placed ourselves before the blackboard, each with a piece of chalk, and placing our hands at the same height I began a slow vertical movement towards the bottom of the board. My pupil did the same, following exactly the same direction, and dividing his attention between his line and mine, his eyes moving constantly from the one to the other as if he wished to verify every point in turn.

The outcome of our work was two exactly parallel lines. My subsequent lessons were merely a development of the same process: I will say no more in this connection. I will add only that by the end of a few months Victor could copy words whose meanings he already knew and very soon afterwards he could reproduce them from memory and finally make use of his writing, shapeless as it was, to express his needs, to ask for the wherewithal to satisfy them and by the same means to understand the needs and wishes of others.

XXXVIII. Considering my experiments a veritable course in imitation, I took care not to limit them purely to acts of manual imitation. I introduced several procedures which had nothing to do with the mechanism of writing but which were much more conducive to the exercise of the intelligence; I drew on the blackboard two circles almost equal in size, one opposite myself and the other opposite Victor. At six or seven points on the circumference of these circles, I wrote six or seven letters of the alphabet: I wrote the same number inside the circles, but arranged them differently. Next, I drew inside one of the circles a series of lines leading to the letters written on the circumference: Victor did exactly the same in his circle. But because the letters were arranged differently, it so happened that even the most accurate imitation produced a figure different from the one I offered him as model. From this developed the idea of a very special kind of imitation which involved not the slavish copying of a given shape, but the reproduction of its style and meaning without being deterred by the difference of the outcome. This was no longer a routine repetition of what the pupil had seen being written, such as some clever animal might be able to produce by imitation, but an intelligent reasoned imitation, as varied in its methods as in its applications, and in a word such as one had the right to expect from a man endowed with the free use of all his intellectual faculties.

XXXIX. Of all the phenomena offered to the observer by a child's early developments, there is none more astonishing than the facility with which he learns to speak; and when one considers that speech is without doubt the most admirable act of imitation and is at the same time its first result, one's admiration is increased for that Supreme Intelligence whose masterpiece is man and who, wishing to make speech the principal force in education, was not able to allow imitation the same progressive development as the other faculties, but had to make it from the very first as active as it was fruitful. But this imitative faculty, whose influence is spread throughout life, varies in its application according to age and is used in learning to speak only at a very early age; later, it directs other functions and abandons the instrument of speech; so that a young child, or even an adolescent, who leaves his native country swiftly loses its manners, life style and language, but never those vocal intonations which constitute what we call the accent. It ensues from this physiological truth that when I awakened the faculty of imitation in our young savage, by now an adolescent, I had no reason to believe that I should find in the organ of speech any disposition to make use of these imitative faculties, even if I had not already found a second obstacle to this in the stubborn torpor of his sense of hearing. In this latter field, Victor could be considered a deaf-mute, though far inferior to that class of sufferers who are essentially observers and imitators.

XL. Nevertheless, I did not wish this difference to bring me to a halt or to force me to abandon all hope of making him speak and thus lose a multitude of advantages – at least, not until I had tried the one last method which remained, namely to lead him to the power of speech not by the sense of hearing, since this seemed to be impossible for him, but by the sense of sight. My last effort involved the exercise of the eyes in understanding the mechanism of articulation and of the voice in repeating sounds with the combined application of attention and imitation. For over a year, all my efforts and all our exercises aimed at this one end. To relate it to my method of gradual progress, I preceded the study of the visible articulation of sounds by the rather easier imitation of the movements of the face muscles, beginning with those most easily seen. Here were teacher and pupil face to face, grimacing as hard as possible, that is to say, exercising the muscles of eyes, forehead, mouth and jaw in every kind of movement; gradually concentrating on the muscles of the lips and after studying carefully and for a very long time the movements of that fleshy part of speech, the tongue, we exercised this in the same way, but more variously and at greater length.

XLI. Thus prepared, it seemed to me that the organ of speech must be ready to lend itself to the imitation of articulated sounds and I considered this outcome imminent and infallible. My hopes were entirely deceived; and all that I could obtain from this long preparation was the emission of meaningless monosyllables, sometimes shrill, sometimes deep and much less clear than those I had obtained in my first experiments. Nevertheless I continued and fought for a long time against the recalcitrance of this organ until finally, realizing that neither the passage of time nor the continuance of my endeavours could effect any change, I resigned myself to giving up my experiments with speech and abandoned my pupil to a life of incurable dumbness.

DEVELOPMENT OF THE EMOTIONAL FACULTIES

XLII. You have seen, my lord, how civilization awoke the intellectual faculties of our savage from their lethargy first by applying them to the satisfaction of his needs, then by extending the scope of his ideas beyond his animal existence. Your Excellency will now see the same order of development in his emotional faculties, first aroused by the feeling of need inspired by the instinct of self-preservation, then stirred by less selfish feelings, by more generous impulses and finally by some of those noble feelings which are the happiness and glory of the human heart.

XLIII. When Victor first entered society, he was insensible to all the care taken of him and, confusing eager curiosity with genuine goodwill, showed no sign of paying any particular attention to the person who looked after him. Approaching her only when forced by necessity and drawing apart when satisfied, he saw her only as a hand that fed him and in that hand he saw only what was held. From the point of view of his moral existence, Victor was only a child in the first days of his life, passing from his mother's breast to that of his nurse, and from her to yet another, finding a difference only in the quantity or quality of the liquid which served him as food. When he came out of his forests, Victor saw the many changes in his keepers with the same indifference and after being cared for most tenderly by a poor Aveyron peasant who showed him a truly fatherly love, he showed no emotion or grief when he was suddenly separated from him.

XLIV. For the first three months of his stay in the Institution, he was harassed by the importunities of the inquisitive as well as by the investigations of those who called themselves interested observers. Wandering in the corridors and gardens of the house in the worst weather of the year, or crouching in corners covered in filth, hungry and alone, he was suddenly taken and cared for by a kindly, loving and wise gouvernante, yet not even this change could arouse in his heart the smallest flicker of gratitude. A pause for thought will show that this was not surprising. How could this gentleness and loving care touch the heart of so impassive a creature? And why should he care about being well-dressed and warm, comfortably lodged and snugly bedded, he who was hardened by the inclemency of the seasons, who cared nothing for the advantages of social life, whose only happiness was freedom, who saw but a prison in the most comfortable of homes?

To arouse his gratitude, he required benefits of quite another order and more likely to be appreciated by his extraordinary nature; to achieve this, it was vital to bow to his tastes and make him happy in his own way. I took this idea as my principal guiding force in the moral treatment of this child. In my first report, I told how I succeeded in arousing his love for his gouvernante and how I made social life bearable for him. His affection, however, lively as it was, could easily have been no more than self-interest. I had reason to suspect this when I noticed that when Victor's gouvernante had been away from him for a few hours or even a few days, Victor hastened to her side with a great show of loving friendship, the intensity of which related not so much to her length of absence as to the very real advantages dependent on her presence, as well as to the deprivations he had endured during the separation. His caresses were no less self-interested and he used them at first to express his wishes rather than show his gratitude, so much so that if one watched carefully as he finished off a copious repast, one could not avoid noticing that he showed every sign of a creature who loses interest in everything around him as soon as his desires are satisfied. However, as time went on, his needs increased and so did our relationships and our cares for his comfort; his stubborn heart opened at last to unmistakable feelings of gratitude and friendship. As proof of this welcome change, I offer two incidents from the many which now occurred.

XLV. The last time our wild boy was tempted to escape from the house by his old memories and his passion for freedom, he ran away towards Senlis and got as far as the forest. It was not long before he emerged from the woods, doubtless driven homewards by hunger and the impossibility of surviving on his own. Once he was in open country, he was arrested by the police and was imprisoned as a vagrant for two weeks. At the end of this time, he was recognized and taken back to Paris; Madame Guérin, his gouvernante, went to collect him at the Temple. A number of inquisitive bystanders gathered to watch their most touching reunion. Scarcely had Victor seen his gouvernante than he turned pale and lost consciousness for a moment; but when he felt her arms around him, he quickly came to his senses and showing his joy by shrill cries, the convulsive clasping of hands and a radiant face, he offered to the eyes of all not so much a fugitive forcibly returned to his keeper as an affectionate son gladly running to the open arms of the one who had given him birth.

XLVI. He showed no less sensibility on his subsequent interview with me. This took place on the following morning. Victor was still in bed and as soon as he saw me, he sat up and held out his arms. But when he saw that instead of going to him I stood where I was with a cold demeanour and an angry face, he dived back beneath the covers and began to cry. I increased his emotion by my reproaches, uttered in a loud and threatening voice; his tears increased and he sobbed long and loud. When I had taken him to the utmost degree of emotion, I sat on the poor penitent's bed. This was always my signal for forgiveness. Victor understood, made the first move of reconciliation and everything was forgiven and forgotten.

XLVII. At about the same time, Madame Guérin's husband fell ill and was nursed outside the home, without Victor's knowledge. One of his small domestic tasks being to lay the table for dinner, he continued to set a place for M. Guérin and though he had every time to remove it, he would always lay it afresh the next day. The illness had a tragic outcome. M. Guérin died and on the very day of his death his place was laid as usual. One can guess the distressing effect this had on Madame Guérin. Witness to this sad scene, Victor understood that he was the cause; and whether he thought he had done wrong or whether he understood the reason for his gouvernante's despair, he realized that his action had been useless and misplaced and of his own accord cleared the place and sadly put the things back in the cupboard. He never laid the place again.

XLVIII. This was a moment of sadness, an emotion belonging entirely to civilized man. Another no less human and civilized is the gloom into which my pupil falls when during the course of our lessons he struggles in vain and with all his attention against some new difficulty which he sees he cannot overcome. It is on such occasions that, filled with the knowledge of his helplessness and touched perhaps by the futility of my efforts, his tears have fallen on those characters he cannot comprehend, without any word of reproach or threat of punishment to provoke his weeping.

XLIX. As civilization increased his moments of sadness, it necessarily also increased his pleasures. I will not discuss those which arose from the satisfaction of his new needs. Although they contributed largely to the development of his emotional faculties, they were, if I may say so, so animal that they could not be accepted as direct proofs of the sensibility of the heart. I will however mention as civilized the zeal he shows and the pleasure he finds in helping the people he loves and even in anticipating their needs, as well as in performing the small services which lie within his scope. One notes this particularly in his relations with Madame Guérin. I will also mention as one of the emotions of a civilized being the satisfaction which spreads over his face, even his outbursts of laughter, when he has been held up in our lessons by some difficulty and he is able at last to overcome it by his own efforts, or when I am sufficiently pleased with his pathetic progress to show him my pleasure by praise and encouragement. It is not only in the experiments that he takes pleasure in doing well, but also in the small domestic tasks which fall to his lot, above all those tasks which demand some muscular effort. For instance, when he is set to saw wood, one can see that when the saw goes deeply into the wood he works harder and harder and at the moment when the wood falls into two sections he shows such extraordinary outbursts of delight that one would be tempted to think him a raving maniac if these tempestuous movements did not have a natural explanation, namely the need for movement in such an active being, and similarly the very nature of the occupation which presents him simultaneously with a healthy exercise, a mechanical action which amuses him and an end result which concerns his needs, all of which combine to offer him in the most obvious way a task both pleasing and useful.

L. But even as the soul of our wild boy gradually opens to some of the pleasures of civilized man, it does not cease to react sensitively to those of his earlier life. He still feels the same passion for the countryside, the same ecstasy at the sight of moonlight and a snow-covered field, the same transports of delight at the sound of a storm wind. His passion for the freedom of the open fields is in fact tempered by frequent open-air walks; but it is a half-extinguished passion and all that is necessary to re-kindle it is a fine summer evening, the sight of a shady wood or the temporary interruption of his daily walks. This latter was the cause of his last escapade. Madame Guérin was kept in bed for a fortnight by an attack of rheumatism and could not take our pupil for his walk. He patiently bore this deprivation for he seemed to understand its cause. But as soon as his gouvernante left her bed, he showed a delight which he grew even more intense when he saw Madame Guérin preparing to go out of doors a few days later; he swiftly got ready to accompany her. She went out without him. He concealed his discontent and when we sent him to the kitchen to bring the dishes to the table at dinner time, he chose a moment when the main gate had been opened to allow a carriage to enter to slip out behind it and run as fast as he could towards the Enfer gate.

LI. The changes brought about by civilization in this young man's soul are not limited to awakening in him emotions and un-expected pleasures; they have also aroused some of those feelings which form what we call righteousness: such is the inner sentiment of justice. Our wild boy was so ignorant of this when he came out of the forests that for a long time afterwards we had to watch care-fully lest he gave way to his insatiable rapacity. However, as one might guess, his need was but a single one, that of hunger, and his thefts were all related to the few foodstuffs he liked to eat. At the beginning he took rather than stole them; and it was with an ease and a touching simplicity that he took them, as though we were back in those distant times when the notion of property had yet to be born in the mind of man. To repress this natural penchant for theft, I punished him whenever I found him stealing. What I gained from this was what society ordinarily obtains from the frightening apparatus of its ultimate punishments, a modification of vice rather than a correction. Victor stole furtively what he had hitherto stolen openly. I thought it wise to try another means of punishment; and to make him feel more keenly the impropriety of his thefts, we had recourse to the law of retaliation. Under this, the strongest law in the world, we punished him by taking away the things he badly wanted – a fruit he had longed for and had earned by good behaviour, small items of food he had stored away in his pockets for future use.

LII. As I expected, these repressive measures were crowned with success and put an end to my pupil's stealing. I did not however imagine that I had inspired the sentiment of justice in his bosom. I was perfectly sure that in spite of the care we had taken to give our confiscations the appearance of a cruel and unjust theft, Victor had probably interpreted them as nothing more than a punishment for his own misdeeds; henceforward, he stood corrected by fear of new deprivations rather than by disinterested feelings of a moral order. To clear my mind on this matter and also to obtain a less equivocal result, I decided to submit my pupil to a test based on another kind of injustice which, being unrelated to the nature of the crime, could not possibly be a well-deserved punishment and because of this was as detestable as it was outrageous. For this truly painful experiment, I chose a day when Victor and I had been working together for more than a couple of hours and when his intelligence and obedience were such that I had only praises and rewards to offer him. To judge from the contented expression of his face and his general demeanour, he was clearly expecting them. Imagine his astonishment when nothing was as he anticipated – there were no rewards and none of my usual demonstrations of pleasure: instead, I put on a severe and threatening expression, rubbed out what I had just praised and scattered all his books and cards around the room. Finally I seized him by the arm and dragged him roughly towards a little dark room which had sometimes served him as a prison when he first came to Paris. He put up no resistance till we got as far as the threshold, then suddenly coming out of his usual submissive state, he put hands and feet against the door posts and set up the most vigorous resistance. This pleased me immeasurably because it was something totally new for him; for when faced by a just punishment, he had always endured it without the slightest air of rebellion. I carried on with my plan, however, as I wished to see how far he would persist in his resistance, and striving my hardest, I tried to pick him up and carry him into the room. This last attempt aroused his full fury. Beside himself with indignation and scarlet with rage, he struggled in my arms with a violence that made all my own efforts quite useless for several minutes: finally, realizing that he could not resist my greater strength for much longer, he used the last resource of the weak; he threw himself on my hand and bit it long and hard. At that moment, I would have given anything to be able to make my pupil understand my act and to tell him that the very pain of his bite filled me with satisfaction and more than rewarded me for my pains! It could only delight me, for the bite was a legitimate act of vengeance; it was an incontestable proof that the idea of justice and injustice, the permanent basis of the social order, was no longer foreign to my pupil's mind. By giving this feeling to him, or rather by stimulating its development, I had raised savage man to the full stature of moral man through the most striking of his characteristics and the most noble of his powers.

LIII. When speaking of the intellectual faculties of our Savage, I have never concealed the obstacles which hindered the development of some of them and I have made it my duty to indicate all the gaps in his intelligence. Following the same plan in the story of his emotions, I shall now reveal the animal part of his nature with the same fidelity that I have used to describe the civilized part. I cannot hide the fact that Victor has remained basically selfish, though he has become responsive to gratitude and friendship and though he seems to enjoy being useful. Eager and happy to help when the services demanded of him are not in opposition to his needs, he is a total stranger to that selfless helpfulness which considers neither deprivations nor sacrifices; the feeling of pity is yet to be born in his heart. If, in his relations with his gouvernante, there have been evidences of sorrow shared, this has been no more than an act of imitation similar to the tears of a child who sees and copies the tears of his mother or his nurse. In order to sympathize with the sorrows of others, one must have experienced them oneself or at least have the power to imagine them. No one can expect this of a young child or of a being like Victor, a stranger to all the pains and privations which compose our moral sufferings.

LIV. But there is something in the emotional system of this young man which is even more astonishing and which defies all explanation: it is his indifference to women, in spite of all the signs and symptoms of a well-developed puberty. I have awaited this moment with great keenness, envisaging it as a source of new sensations for my pupil and of fascinating observations for myself, watching out carefully for all the preliminary phenomena of this moral crisis; every day, I waited for a breath of that universal emotion which stirs and stimulates all creatures, expecting it to move Victor in his turn and enlarge his moral existence. I have seen the arrival – or rather, the explosion – of this long-desired puberty, seen our Savage consumed by desires of an extreme violence and a fearful continuity without once realizing their purpose or feeling any form of preference for any woman. Instead of that burst of enthusiasm which urges one sex towards the other, he has shown only a sort of blind instinct, a rather indistinct preference which makes the society of women more agreeable to him than the company of men, but without actually experiencing any true emotion in this connection. I have seen him sometimes in the company of women, trying to find some solace for his feelings by sitting next to some young lady and gently squeezing her arms, hands and knees, carrying on thus until his restless desires were increased rather than calmed by these strange caresses; and then, unable to see an end to these painful emotions, suddenly change and angrily thrust aside she whom he had eagerly sought, only to turn to yet another in his search for fulfilment. One day, however, he took his endeavours a little further. After a few preliminary caresses, he took the lady by the hand and pulled her – though without violence – into a small alcove.

There, he seemed at a loss to know what to do next, his face and behaviour revealed a curious mixture of gaiety and sadness, boldness and uncertainty, and finally he tried to persuade the lady to caress him by offering her his cheeks; he walked round and round her thoughtfully and then threw his arms round her shoulders and hugged her tightly. This was all he did and the demonstrations of love came to an end, like all the others, with a burst of vexation which made him push away the object of his transitory desires.

LV. Since this period, the unfortunate young man has been no less tormented by the tumult of the senses, but he no longer seeks solace in these useless caresses. However, his apparent resignation has not served to make his condition more bearable: on the contrary, it has exasperated him and made him find a reason for despair in his failure, since he cannot hope to satisfy his needs. When this tumult of the senses bursts upon us, it serves no purpose to have cold baths, a soothing diet or violent exercise; his naturally sweet temper is transformed and passing swiftly from sadness to anxiety and from anxiety to fury, he turns against the things he most likes, sighs, weeps, utters shrill cries, tears his clothes and sometimes even goes so far as to scratch or bite his gouvernante. But even when he is prey to a blind and uncontrollable fury, he still feels a genuine remorse and wants to kiss the arm or hand he has bitten. When he is in this state, his pulse is raised, his face red and swollen; sometimes blood flows from his nose and ears, which ends the outburst and postpones its repetition, especially if the haemorrhage is copious. Going on from this particular observation, I would add that I have sometimes had to bleed him to calm him down, but always with great caution because I am convinced that it is better to mitigate this effervescence than to extinguish it completely. But I should say at the same time that if I have obtained a little calm by the use of this method and a wide variety of others too various to mention, the effect has never been more than temporary and this continuity of violent yet unsatisfied desires has led to a habitual state of restless suffering and anxiety which has constantly hindered the already slow and difficult progress of his education.

LVI. This was the critical period which was so promising and which would doubtless have fulfilled all the hopes we had attached to it if, instead of restricting its influence solely to the senses, it had managed to stimulate his moral system equally and carry the flame of passion into his torpid heart. I will not hide the fact, though, that serious reflection has led me to the conclusion that when I counted on this particular mode of development in the phenomena of puberty, I was wrong to compare my pupil to an ordinary adolescent whose love for women often precedes or at least accompanies the excitement of the sex organs. This concordance of needs and desires could not possibly be found in a creature who had not been taught to distinguish between men and women and who had to rely on instinct alone to grasp the difference between them, without ever being able to usefully apply whatever knowledge he might have gained. I did not doubt but that if I had dared to reveal the secret of his anxieties and the reason for his desires to this young man I would have reaped an incalculable benefit. But on the other hand, supposing that I could have tried such an experiment, would I not have revealed to our Savage a need which he would doubtless have sought to satisfy as publicly as his other needs and which would have led him into acts of great indecency? The fear of such an outcome inhibited my further experiments and I resigned myself to seeing my hopes disappear here, as on so many other occasions, before an unforeseen obstacle.

This, my lord, is the story of the changes that have taken place in the emotional system of the Savage of Aveyron. This section terminates all the facts relating to the development of my pupil over a period of four years. Many of the facts speak in favour of his possible improvement whilst others suggest the contrary. I have made it my duty to present them all impartially and to recount my failures as well as my successes. The astonishing variety in the results make it impossible to reach any firm conclusion on Victor and casts a sort of disharmony into the consequences one might draw from the facts related in this memoir. Thus, gathering together those scattered through paragraphs VI, VII, XVIII, XX, XLI, LIII and LIV, one must conclude: (1) that following on the almost total absence of speech and hearing, the young man's education is still and always will be incomplete; (2) that because of their long period of inactivity, his intellectual faculties can develop only slowly and with difficulty and that this development, which among children raised in a civilized society is the natural outcome of time and circumstances, is here the slow and arduous result of an active education where the most forceful methods have been used to obtain the slightest results; (3) that the emotions, emerging with equal slowness from their long torpor, are subordinated in their application to a deep feeling of selfishness and that puberty instead of effecting a tremendous emotional development seems to exist here only to prove that if there exists in man a relationship between the needs of the senses and the emotions of the heart, then this sympathetic harmony is, like most great and noble passions, the fortunate fruit of man's education.

But if I recapitulate the happy changes in this young man's condition, and in particular the facts listed in paragraphs IX, X, XI, XII, XIV, XXI, XXV, XXVII, XXX, XXXI, XXXII, XXXIII, XXXIV,

XXXV, XXXVII, XXXVIII, XLIV, XLV, XLVI, XLVII and XLIX, one must of necessity see his education in a more favourable light and accept the following conclusions: (1) that the improvement in touch and sight and the newly acquired pleasures of taste have, by multiplying the sensations and ideas of our Savage, contributed very largely to the development of his intellectual faculties; (2) that when his overall development is considered, we find among other improvements the knowledge of the conventional meaning of the symbols of thought, and the power to apply this knowledge by indicating objects, their properties and their actions, whence the extension of the pupil's relations with people around him, the faculty of communicating his needs, taking orders and constantly exchanging thoughts; (3) that in spite of his immoderate liking for the freedom of the open country and his indifference to most of the niceties of social life, Victor is now grateful for the care that is taken of him, is capable of an affectionate friendship, is responsive to the pleasures of doing well, is ashamed of his mistakes and repentant of his outbursts; (4) that finally, my lord, from whatever point of view one looks at this long experiment, whether one sees it as the methodical education of a wild man, or whether one restricts oneself to considering it as the physical and moral treatment of one of those creatures born ill-favoured, rejected by society and abandoned by medicine, the care that has been lavished on him, the care that is still his due, the changes that have taken place, those one hopes are still to come, the voice of humanity, the interest aroused by so cruel a desertion and so strange a fate, all these things combine to commend this extraordinary young man to the attention of scholars, the solicitude of our administrators and the protection of the government.

Translated by Joan White

Details of some
other titles
published by NLB
will be found
on the following pages

The Concept of Nature in Marx

Alfred Schmidt

Translated from the German by Ben Fowkes

The central importance of Marx's concept of nature in the formulation of historical materialism has been almost totally neglected in the English language literature on Marx, despite the fact that it is crucial for an understanding both of the 'materialist conception of history' (is it 'materialist' in the philosophical sense?) and of the dialectic (is the dialectic an objective process or an instrument of the human mind?).

Schmidt's close reading of Marx's own writings from all periods of his life and particularly from the Grundrisse, and his discussion of Marx's positions in relation to those of Kant, Hegel, Engels, Lenin, the early Lukács, Sartre and others, enables him to establish the significance of the mature Marx's sense of the interpenetration of nature and society. He shows how Marxism thus cuts right across the traditional tendency to counterpose an abstract concept of man with an abstract concept of nature. Schmidt stresses the importance in Marxism of the development of industry and science as the mediation between historical man and external nature, leading either to their reconciliation (if positive) or to their mutual annihilation (if negative). He then both explores this mediation in history and shows how an awareness of its positive and negative possibilities is reflected in such writers as Bertolt Brecht, Walter Benjamin and Ernst Bloch.

£3.25

Immanuel Kant

Lucien Goldmann

Translated from the French and German by Robert Black

This book is one of the few studies of Kant's philosophy which considers it as a whole. Lucien Goldmann investigates the relation between the critical and pre-critical periods in the development of Kant's thought and argues that the widespread neglect of the latter has inhibited a proper understanding of the former. Kant's search for a concept of totality is seen as the unifying theme of his philosophy.

Goldmann places Kant's ideas in their social and historical context. It was in this work that Goldmann laid the basis for his use of the theme of the 'tragic vision', later developed in his remarkable study of Pascal and Racine, *The Hidden God*. Goldmann insists that Kant's philosophy of religion was a disguised philosophy of history which could readily be emancipated from its theological trappings. By contrasting Kant's vision of totality with the radically different world view of English empiricism and French rationalism, Goldmann establishes the nature of Kant's special and decisive contribution to the development of European philosophy. In doing so he shows why Hegel, Marx and Lukács regarded Kant's thought as the philosophical complement to the French revolution.

£2.90

Marxism and Philosophy

Karl Korsch

Translated from the German by Fred Halliday

Karl Korsch's *Marxism and Philosophy* is one of the most famous works produced by the European revolutionary movement. It appeared in the same year as George Lukács's *History and Class Consciousness* and was the object of even greater debate and attack. The reasons why are still evident today.

 Marxism and Philosophy is the first attempt by a Marxist to apply Marx's critical and materialist method to the history of Marxism itself. It discusses the evolution of Marx's own thought during his lifetime, and the crisis of the orthodox theory of the pre-1914 Social Democracy which led to the formation of the Third International. Korsch argued that ideology was a crucial instrument of bourgeois society, and that Marxists must struggle against it just as they fight its economic and political structures.

 Marxism and Philosophy was eventually condemned by the Comintern. Unlike Lukács, Korsch did not accept Party discipline, and in 1930 he replied to his critics in a trenchant Anti-Critique, included in this volume. In the revival of Marxist theory in Western Europe over the past decade, Korsch's work has played a major role.

£2.00

Sexuality and Class Struggle

Reimut Reiche

Translated from the German by Susan Bennett

This book which combines the methods and results of both Marx and Freud is by one of the leaders of the West German left during its most militant phase in the late 1960s.

For reasons the author makes clear, the anti-authoritarian movement took more thoroughgoing and trenchant forms in West Germany than anywhere else. A new sexual morality was not only preached but practised. Is it possible, however – the author asks – that this new emphasis on sexual enlightenment and liberty can become merely a characteristic of Western capitalism, which serves to activate the market economy, deflect rebellion, and hence contribute to the preservation of the system? In answering this question Reiche explains and develops Marcuse's widely misunderstood theory of 'repressive desublimation'. He exposes the artificial and illusory nature of many attempts – in Germany and elsewhere – at 'sexual liberation', and shows why it is impossible to overcome sexual oppression and mystification in our society in isolation from the political struggle.

£2.00

A Short History of the European Working Class

Wolfgang Abendroth

Translated from the German by Nicholas Jacobs and Brian Trench

At a time when the interests of the European working class are ever more visibly linked, this is the first study to give an outline history of the working-class movement as a whole – in West and East Europe, from the industrial revolution and the formation of the urban proletariat, to modern times.

Describing and analysing the most important social, political and economic struggles of the working-class movement in different countries, the author has charted the general trajectory and gauged the momentum of a movement which has at times been at a standstill and at others has, in the words of Karl Marx, 'stormed the gates of heaven'. Focusing especially but by no means exclusively on the French, German, Russian and British movements, Abendroth shows the particular contribution each has made to the movement as a whole.

At decisive turning-points of European history – in the Revolutions of 1848, in the Paris Commune of 1871, in the Bolshevik Revolution of 1917, and in the victory over Fascism in 1944–5 – the working class has shown itself to be potentially the most powerful and creative single factor in modern European history. In showing how the working class has used that power in the past, this book is a pointer towards its use in the immediate future.

£2.50

Karl Marx

Werner Blumenberg

Translated from the German by Douglas Scott

This book is the first of its kind on Marx in English. It not only contains reproductions of virtually every picture of Marx and his family in existence, but is illustrated by a uniquely wide set of quotations, from his early school essays and attempts at romantic poetry to his mature works and vast correspondence with Engels. This material is linked by a lucid text which narrates the facts of Marx's life and explains the significance of each stage of his intellectual output and political activity.

No biography before has portrayed in such detail Marx's relationship with his mother and father, studied here with generous quotations from their letters as well as his own. Marx's relationship with his own family and friends, the often cruel hardship of his life in London, the apparent contradictions in his work, all are studied for the light they throw on a man whose influence changed the course of history – of whom, when he was only twenty-four, a friend wrote: 'Imagine Rousseau, Voltaire, Holbach, Lessing, Heine and Hegel united in one person, and I say *united*, not just thrown together – then you've got Dr Marx.'

£2.50 (hardback)   .85p (paperback)